Readings in Child Development
Second Edition

A. Lynn Scoresby
Alvin H. Price
Brigham Young University

McGraw-Hill, Inc.
College Custom Series

New York St. Louis San Francisco Auckland Bogotá
Caracas Hamburg Lisbon London Madrid Mexico Milan Montreal
New Delhi Paris San Juan São Paulo Singapore Sydney Tokyo Toronto

McGraw-Hill's **College Custom Series** consists of products that are produced from camera-ready copy. Peer review, class testing, and accuracy are primarily the responsibility of the author(s).

READINGS IN CHILD DEVELOPMENT

Copyright © 1992, by McGraw-Hill, Inc. All rights reserved. Printed in the United States of America. Except as permitted under the United States Copyright Act of 1976, no part of this publication may be reproduced or distributed in any form or by any means, or stored in a data base retrieval system, without prior written permission of the publisher.

3 4 5 6 7 8 9 0 MALMAL 9 0 9 8 7 6 5 4 3

ISBN 0-07-055963-5

Editor: Jon K. Earl

Cover Design: Janet Spring

Printer/Binder: Malloy Lithographing, Inc

READINGS IN

CHILD DEVELOPMENT

A. Lynn Scoresby

&

Alvin H. Price

TABLE OF CONTENTS

Concepts of Child Development 1

Theories of Child Development 5

Innate Needs 12

Principles of Development 27

Learning Disability 34

Perception 41

Individual Differences 46

The Brain and The Nervous System in Child Development 50

Moral Conduct 65

Friendship 69

Emotions in Children 74

Social Language 79

Why Children Do What They Do 84

Teaching Children About Sex and Reproduction 91

Culture and Child Development 99

Rules 103

A Dysfunctional Family 108

The Endocrine Glands 115

Families As Socializers 127

Child Observation 135

Self-Regulation 137

A Practical Identity 141

Identity Formation 146

The Development of Independence 151

Dating and Courtship 156

Delinquency 161

Sex Roles 166

A Self-Esteem Inventory 170

Your Style of Learning and Thinking 172

Interpersonal Reasoning 173

Development of Adolescent Peer Groups 177

Achievement Motivation 184

CONCEPTS OF DEVELOPMENT

Behavioral scientists have studied many aspects of human behavior. This concentrated effort by thousands of researchers and writers has yielded much useful and significant information about human development. In spite of all that has been done, there is one condition or variable which has not been well researched. It is the factor of time and how it influences what we are.

In a general way, or course, we have some theories which suggest that events early in life influence what happens later. But for the most part, we still have difficulty trying to understand how time becomes part of and influences the human personality.

The matter of time is of increased importance when we focus on human development. Development takes place over time and scientists suggest that it is orderly instead of random and confused. Further, development appears to have a direction of some sort which means it has a goal or objective. Lastly, some believe that development is continuous and others suggest that it is sporadic. Regardless of which position you accept, however, none of these ideas are useful if one does not see and understand them related to time.

As a practical matter we are interested in what happens to a child of any age during certain segments of time. We want to know what happens, what causes it to happen, and what might influence it. Why? For one thing, we are interested in these questions from the point of view of any scientist. Development is significant and studying about it may improve the human condition. Development sometimes is not successful. It can be adversely affected by many things. For those who guide children such as parents, teachers, physicians, and church leaders, knowledge about ineffective development is essential.

You can imagine observing a child and noticing something interesting or unusual about him. Let's suppose you notice a four year old playing and having fun in the living room of your house. Then, you put on his coat and put him in the car to run a few errands. To your surprise, instead of being pleasant, he begins to whine, say mean words, and tease his little sister. From your point of view, you are annoyed with what he is doing. Should you spank him, yell at him, or ignore what is happening? What you do will depend on how you interpret this event. Is it just the changeability one expects from a four year old? Is it that the child does not like cars? Is he a big tease and likes to torment? Or, is it a manifestation of something that is developmental? If you are unaware of it being developmental you might spank or scold. What if you know that before three children do not have a concept of rules and then they begin to think rules are part of every situation. Four year old children are very interested in rules, and when they do not know them, they will misbehave in order to find out. Knowing this developmental information, you will neither spank nor scold. You will take the time to teach your child the rules for riding in a car. You may also have a good time doing it and then all you will need to do is remind him.

THE HUMAN DESIGN

Probably the best way to understand development over time is to understand something about the idea that humans have built-in or inherited mechanisms for both time and development. Inside the brain we can find a small mechanism that moves much like a clock. It actually rocks and keeps pace with time. New development takes place after certain amounts of time have passed and been measured by the brain's mechanism. In addition, microbiologists have found "master" genes on some chromosomes which control the expression of other genes. These lie dormant until certain time has passed and then act to signal other genes which influence further development.

In addition to these two examples which appear to be built-in features of brain and body, other conditions exist which stimulate and are a manifestation of development. All infants, for example, demonstrate an orienting response which allows them to move, or orient their body in order to take full advantage of the world around them. This has the net effect of adding stimulation which promotes their development. Every infant also demonstrates an inherited "competency motivation" or drive to improve physical and mental skills. This motivation is evidenced by children's drive to turn over, crawl, walk, and run. And, it is manifest by a child's drive to learn language and acquire new mental skills.

ENLARGEMENT AND INTEGRATION

Generally, as time passes and development takes place, an individual's capacity for thoughts, feelings, and skills are enlarged. One who is more mature, thinks more thoughts, feels more and more refined emotional characteristics, and can do more complex skills than the one who is less mature. Knowing this you can expect yourself and your children to think more effectively and develop emotionally as you and they grow.

While this enlargement gradually appears, another form of development is also happening. It is called integration. This means that as the brain matures it increases its capacity to collect information and integrate it into increasingly complex understandings. A young person could tell one person apart from others and that individuals belong to families. It would take a more mature child to understand that families are part of towns which are part of cities, counties, states, countries, worlds and solar systems. It would take a fairly integrated mind to know the various ways all these parts may be related or connected to one another.

What does this mean to you? If you understand that humans develop over time then you will have an enlarged capacity for understanding children and yourself. Further, you will see your ideas about children become more integrated and your treatment of them will come closer to their situation in time. Collectively, if we all improve our understanding of development, we can improve our ability to rear children until they become humane, responsible, and mature adults.

LEARNING ACTIVITIES

Objective: To increase your understanding of development as it takes place over time.

1. Interview two people asking and recording their answers to the following questions: (these questions are designed to learn how much people might or might not know about development)

    a. Describe something you have improved as you have matured. _____
    _____

    b. What would you do if a four year old child began to tease, whine, and cry while you were driving a car? _____
    _____

    c. What is the best thing to do if your first grad child cannot read well? _____
    _____

    d. Describe how a ten year old might learn differently than a five year old. __
    _____

2. In the following types of development, describe how you have enlarged your ability.

    a. physical _____

    b. language _____

    c. emotional _____

    d. social _____

    e. cognitive _____

3. Write a behavioral description of the typical actions for a young child, a teenager, a young adult, and a mature adult. _____
_____
_____
_____
_____
_____
_____

THEORIES OF CHILD DEVELOPMENT

Years ago doctors were attempting to learn how diseases spread. Not knowing about bacteria they developed a theory based on what they thought they knew and what they observed. Imagine what preventative strategies they arrived at when they first thought that infections were spread by the wind. Their advice was to keep children from drafts and ill people away from fresh air. After discovering the idea of contagion by air they thought perhaps the cause was the smell of illness. They supported this idea by the idea that when ill people in hospitals were separated from one another, meaning they could not smell sickness, there was less transmission of disease. Bacteria in the role of infection was discovered in a hospital where doctors realized they were spreading it by using unsterilized surgical instruments. The first people operated on did not get the same illnesses as those who had later operations. Someone noticed this, realized it must be due to something going on in the operating room and suspected the cause of infectious disease was something they could not see. Then later, with the development of the microscope, the existence of bacteria was confirmed.

Researchers studying child development and human behavior started out with ideas as strange as the thought that smell causes disease. These early ideas were useful though because they could be disproved. This led to progressively better ideas until our present time. We now know that we do not know everything, there may be very new and exciting discoveries made about children, and that we should be open to learning about them. However, for you who are new to the study of child development, it is important to learn about what has been and is thought about children so that you can use these ideas to generate or understand new discoveries.

THEORIES ARE THE BEGINNING

Everybody uses theories. You may have some idea about how to get a date, the best way to buy a car, how to make friends, or how to get money from your parents. They are part of everyday life and are so common you probably give them little thought. Your theories will be good or bad depending on whether they work the way you hope. When they work, (i.e. you get a date) you conclude your theory is a good one. When desired results are not obtained (i.e. you cannot make friends) you will revise your theory by first questioning what went wrong, getting some new information, and then trying again.

This same process is an on going effort in the study of human behavior. Researchers try things out, if they seem to work, the theory seems to be a good one, if they fail the theory is revised.

In our case, we are especially interested in those theories which are used to explain child development. So as you begin your study, you should understand what a theory is. A theory is an organized and focussed set of ideas. Since humans are so complex, a theory narrows what we are able to observe. One theory, for example, might focus on observable external behavior while another might focus our attention on inward thoughts or feelings. (1) Theories have original or "a priori" assumptions which are the beginning or orginating ideas for the theory. (2) A theory describes a "behavioral domain." This is usually fine in a set of terms or vocabulary which explain what one sees when child behavior is observed. The word "maturation" refers to growth determined by biological factors while "learning" refers to growth determined by children's experience with their environment. (3) Besides a vocabulary that identifies a behavioral domain, a theory also contains predictions which are used to predict what causes growth and what can be expected in the future. For instance we can predict that all human beings will mature and go through puberty, a time of rapid biological growth. (4) Theories are not a set of wild ideas. Theories are partially proven systems of thought which are supported by much research but still contain some unproven ideas called hypotheses. These hypotheses are the exciting parts of theories because they are at the forefront of knowledge where scientists are working to confirm or disconfirm how children develop. Each theory proposes methods of proving or disproving them.

FOUR THEORIES

When you study a theory it is important for you to learn about its assumptions and then you can tell where it started and how researchers and writers have developed the theory over the years. In addition, you can find out what part of human behavior the theory is going to focus on and what part it is not. Consider the following.

BEHAVIOR THEORIES

This theory begins with the assumption that humans inherit some survival drives such as hunger, thirst, sex, and perhaps curiosity. When individuals seek to satisfy these drives (to survive) they learn. This learning is based on two laws: the law of association and the law of effect. When we attempt to satisfy our hunger we learn all we can about what is associated with food and our bodily response to food. This is the law of association. We also learn what will get us food (i.e. money). Thus we will learn what we must do to get money in order to get food. This is the law of effect.

Behavior theories focus on external behavior. They contain words which direct us to understand a stimulus and response, to count the frequency of some act or how some action may be reinforced or extinguished. In addition, they try to explain what external actions are related or associated with certain emotions.

PSYCHOANALYTIC THEORIES

Psychoanalytic theories begin with the assumption that humans inherit certain mental and emotional characteristics. These inherited tendencies develop in a sequence of age stages. This means that at certain ages children will manifest certain mental and emotional characteristics. A second assumption is that the rate of development can be affected by the nature of one's exposure to the environment. That is, any new thoughts or feelings are largely affected or determined by the type of experience in our past. For example, if our parents were mean to us we might be afraid and later assume that all people will hurt us. As time passes, and we collect our life experiences, all development is due to the "interaction" of inherited characteristics and these experiences.

Psychoanalytic theories focus on emotions and thoughts. The words of these theories describe the inward part of human behavior and consider systems of thought and feeling to be the most important parts of development.

COGNITIVE THEORIES

These theories begin with the assumptions that humans inherit a brain structure which determines certain styles of thought or cognition. It is proposed, for example, that cognitive development takes place in some age stages and is affected by how rich or limited one's interaction is with the environment. The richer our exposure the better and more elaborate will be our ability to think and reason.

Cognitive theories describe several different mental activities or "cognitive operations" and are used to explain or predict what will happen at certain ages of growth and what will help or hurt development. (e.g. neglect will hinder development while much positive exposure to people and objects will help children grow).

ETHOLOGICAL THEORIES

Ethological theories have assumptions which are different than any of the other three. These theories start with the assumption that human development stems from inherited characteristics. Further, ethological theories focus on the behavior which one exhibits toward other members of its species. These include eating, mating, survival, parenting, and play behavior. According to these theories, all individuals inherit the behavior which allow them to participate in these tasks. Therefore, they show how to observe the behavior of one individual and compare it to the actions of other species members.

These theories contain words which direct attention toward external behavior but as it is related to the species' tasks. Mating in humans would be an example of the focus demonstrated by ethological theories. Advocates of this theory are also interested in how individuals grow into demonstration of the types of behaviors related to the species tasks.

THEORIES AND YOUR UNDERSTANDING OF CHILD DEVELOPMENT

Each of the four theories described above enable us to refine our abilities to understand children. You may like one more than you do any others. But, it is important to remember that each has its value by focusing our attention of different aspects of child development and by giving us different ways to think about children. We are probably better informed if we are familiar with all four theories than if we know none or only one. Therefore, you will be asked to be knowledgeable about all four theories of child development.

As you study these theories, notice they will help you decide what you think. These theories can, in fact, help you develop your own theory about children and how they develop. You might never become a researcher or a scientist in a formal sense. But, you might become a parent or a teacher. Do you think it is important to have a theory about children and how they develop? What if your theory is too limited and you have some notions which are not true? What will the consequences be for the children? What if you have a variety of ways to think about a child? Will you likely do a better job of understanding and predicting what the child will do?

The answers to these questions are pretty obvious aren't they? This implies, however, that as you acquire knowledge about these theories and about children that you should examine your assumptions and that you should decide what parts of human behavior you want to consider. Are you more interested in observable external behavior than you are in mental development? Or are you equally concerned about thoughts, emotions, and acts?

The theories provide a way to understand and also provide specific knowledge about children. You can use them to formulate your own theory and in so doing improve your ability to promote healthy human development.

LEARNING ACTIVITIES

Objective: To refine your understanding of theories and the role theories play in understanding children and in the formulation of your own theory of child development.

1. What are the four characteristics of a theory?
   a. _____
   b. _____
   c. _____
   d. _____

2. Answer the following questions about the four theories.
   a. Which theories are stage theories? _____
   b. Which theories assume development is mostly due to what is inherited? _____
   c. Which theory or theories focus exclusively on learning? _____
   d. Which theories focus on development which results from interaction between the individual and the environment? _____

3. What aspect of human behavior does each theory focus on?
   a. Behavioral theories _____
   b. Psychoanalytic theories _____
   c. Cognitive theories _____
   d. Ethological theories _____

4. After completing the exercises listed above, begin to develop your own theory.
   a. Read the following statements and select one as your "a priori" assumption.
      1. Children are born and are like blank pages ready to be filled by what they experience and learn. Who they eventually become is up to their parents, other caring people, and experiences children choose themselves. A child's growth is due to learning and experiencing.

2. Children are born full of genetic potential that affects all they do. Who they eventually become is determined in large part by their inherited characteristics. A child's growth is due to inherited possibilities.

b. Select one of these two statments. Using your knowledge of the four theories provide support for the one position you selected.

c. By now you have some thoughts about what you believe. State two "a priori" assumptions you have about development and then support your ideas with logical reasons derived from the four theories or your own experience. Be specific and use examples to illustrate your ideas.

NOTE: This paper should be about four pages in length. Use sub-headings to organize your paper. Be grammatically correct.

INNATE NEEDS

The root that nourishes all human relationships is the principle of stewardship. Stewardship is a charge to care for and nurture others. Stewardship implies an accounting to someone. Sometimes we are accountable to entities in this life. Parents often have to account for their stewardship to schools, welfare agencies, churches, and the law. For instance, if parents are not good stewards and neglect children, the state may take the children out of the home and place them in foster care. It always comes as a shock to students to find out that legally their children do not belong to them. They belong to the state in which they live. You could test this notion out. Abuse a child and see what happens. If the state knows about it, the child will be taken away from you while people try to train you to be more nurturant. If you can't or won't change your behavior then your child might be permanently taken from you. So legally, children don't belong to parents. This means parents can't do whatever they want to with their children. Neither do children belong to parents theologically. Most major religions believe that children belong to God, who has expectations of what parents should do with His children.

To be a good steward over children, a person has to accept the notion that each child is unique. It is unfair for parents to think all their children are the same and try to fit all of them into the same mold. The uniqueness of children comes from several sources. First, children are unique because of their genetic inheritance. Everyone is genetically different, unless they have an identical twin. Science is just beginning to discover some of the subtle personality traits that heredity influences. For instance, whether a person is impulsive or reflective seems to largely be determined by genes.

The second source of uniqueness comes from the environment. The environment includes everything that happens to a person from the moment they are conceived. <u>Everyone</u> has had a unique environment. It is impossible to create the same environment for two people. Sometimes parents of twins try to make their children's lives identical, but it is impossible. They can dress them alike, give them names that sound alike, and even put them side by side in a double-seated stroller so that they go through life seeing new things at the same time, but their environment is still not the same.

Most children do the same things over a long period of time. All children get angry with their parents, they all have temper tantrums and negative behavior. Children do the same things, but not at the same time. Child "A" has a talent for throwing a temper tantrum just as the family comes home from church when everyone is feeling pretty mellow. The mother says to herself, "I can understand this behavior, he's just growing up. Bless his little heart. He's in a stage. He'll grow out of it." The behavior of child "A" is seen through rose-colored glasses by the mother. But another child, Child "B" does the same thing five minutes before his mother has an appointment. His temper tantrum makes her late. The mother interprets the behavior, which is the same as Child "A," through different-colored glasses and reacts to him differently. Then an interesting thing happens. The mother starts to see Child "B" as a bad child and she "tunes-into" bad behaviors more often or interprets more and more of that child's behavior as bad. She may label the child as bad and then look for confirmation in his behavior. And she can find it. She will ignore the good things that the child does. Some of you know what I am talking about because you were assigned such a label in your family. The opposite happens with Child "A." Once a parent gives a child a label, the other brothers and sisters catch on and they use the label. Check this out. Next time your family gathers together, have everyone write down three adjectives that describe each person. You might be surprised at how much agreement there is among your brothers and sisters. Usually everyone in a family knows the role that they and everyone else is supposed to play. This happens with both good and bad traits.

Every text discusses the influences of heredity and environment at great length, but fails to discuss a third major factor that contributes to a child's uniqueness--a child's spirit. Psychologists do not like to talk about the spirit of man. And because they don't, they can't explain some important things in human development. The spirit of a person had an existence before the person was born. While psychologists won't talk about the spirit, they have observed that there is something besides heredity and environment that contributes to the personality of an individual. Freud, for instance, called it the Id.

Poets have also had this insight about the spirit. Here is a section of a poem by Wordsworth, which suggests an independent pre-earth existence of people's spirits:

> Our birth is but a sleep and a forgetting.
> The soul that rises with us
> Our life's star
> Hath had elsewhere its setting
> And cometh from afar.
> Not in entire forgetfulness
> And not in utter nakedness
> But trailing clouds of glory do we come
> From God who is our home.

That force which others have hesitated to label, we believe to be the spirit of man.

An understanding of the concept of the spirit can help us realize how children are both unique and similar. All spirits existed and developed in another environment before they became part of a human on earth. In that prior existence, spirits developed in the same way that mortals do here on earth. They learned things, they had social relationships, and they developed personalities. Just as in this life there are big differences in people's abilities, so there were differences in how spirits developed. One of the places where there was a wide range of differences was in the types of personalities that were formed. When a baby is born here on earth, the spirit which gives him life has a personality and that personality starts to show itself.

An infant is very immature. He has few voluntary movements which he can make and he has limited intellectual ability. He is essentially a reflexive organism, and responds to his environment through a series of reflexes. Because of the immaturity of the infant, it is not possible to see fine gradations of personality. However, nearly all parents and close observers of children have noticed that there are several different basic innate personality types in children. They can describe the difference but they cannot explain them. Those types seem to be present from the moment of birth and thus cannot be explained by environmental factors. But different temperaments can easily be explained by realizing that spirits had quite different personalities when they became part of a living person. These personalities begin to interact with people in the environment at birth, and may change quite a bit over a child's lifetime. For some people this explanation may seem to lack scientific rigor, but it is no less rigorous than other psychologist's explanations. Infant predispositions is an area where it is impossible to do research. This explanation is simple and fits with the things that the world has observed in children, and no one can refute it. It could be the true explanation.

The concept of the spirit can also help us understand how all children are similar. It has been observed by many psychologists that children are born with similar needs--internal forces that push them to seek similar goals. These have been called innate needs. Innate needs have been found to be the same in all children in every culture. They are independent of the culture in which a child is raised. Children do not acquire these needs; they are born with them. But they do not come from the child's genes. These needs cannot be accounted for by environmental or genetic factors. So where do they come from? Again the concept of the spirit gives us a simple, clear, and we think, true explanation. In its pre-earth existence each spirit gained knowledge about what its ultimate destiny could be. The spirit knew that it would inhabit a body and eventually exit that body in what we call death. The spirit knew that it would continue to exist, not in the sense that it would be recycled into another body to repeat again an earthly experience, but exist in another environment that we know little of. Some people call this Heaven. The spirit knew that if it developed in certain ways in its earthly existence, it would be a help later in its post-earthly existence. Since all spirits have a knowledge of, and seek the same ultimate goal, shouldn't they be seeking for similar experiences in this life, no matter what culture they were born into? If they did, this would explain why we see the same kinds of strivings in children.

The list of innate needs, those strivings that came with the spirit, is not lengthy. They are usually not related to the needs which a society says one should seek for. A need of the spirit should meet the following criteria. First, all people in all cultures will manifest that need. It does not matter if you are born to an Eskimo mother or a Guatemalan Indian mother. It does not matter if you are born today or a thousand years ago, or 1500 years B.C., when Moses was crossing the Red Sea. If all children in all cultures in all historic periods have the same need, it is a need of the spirit. Secondly, if something is a true need of the spirit, people will never outgrow that need. We should be able to see the need in both children and their parents.

Each of these innate needs is like an empty milk bucket that needs to be filled. When the bucket or need is full, a person is happy. Unfortunately, every bucket has a hole in the bottom. No matter how often it is filled, if a parent relaxes and thinks, "Well, that is taken care of," and stops filling the bucket, then the bucket will eventually drain dry, and the child will seek to satisfy the unmet need.

Suppose that for lunch someday someone takes you to the local Taco Bell. You eat four burritos, which should fill up anybody. And then this person orders four more for you to eat. You eat one more but can't eat the rest and so this person forces you to eat the other three burritos. At this point you say, "One more bite and I will throw up!" this person asks, "Are you full?" And you say, "YES!" And I say, "Good, no more food for a month." You know that won't work. Your bucket for physical food is overflowing, but in three days, you will be hungry again. The same analogy holds for each of the needs we are going to discuss. They need constant replenishment.

When a need is not filled, some interesting things happen. First, the spirit knows that something is wrong, and at a subconscious level it tries to give the child a message to do something. It can't whisper in an ear, but it tries to bring about change. Sometimes it does this through attention-getting behavior. Some believe that most of the hyperactivity in elementary school children is caused by one or more of their innate needs not being met. When children act out, they are sending a message to teachers and parents that they need help. If the non-directed attention-getting behavior does not work because others ignore them, then a second event usually happens. The spirit inside the child gives up and a depression sets in.

Many adults have grown up with some of their needs only partially filled and, as a result, are not totally healthy in some area of their development, such as intellectual, moral, or social development. Adults can fill their own buckets; they can heal themselves. If a person feels he is intellectually stunted, he can take a class and learn something new. If a person is physically out of shape, she can take up jogging or aerobics and get in shape. Adults <u>can</u> fill their own needs. Only in the most severe cases of neglect might a person need help from someone else, such as a physician, counselor, teacher, or minister. You cannot fill another person's bucket if your own is dry. Parents should make sure they are healthy before they start to work on their children. If they are not healthy, they may not even be able to see the needs that their children have. In childhood, some buckets have such big holes that the buckets have to be filled up every day.

Let's discuss some of the important innate needs. This list is not exhaustive but includes most of the currently recognized innate needs. The first need is the need to stay alive. This is perhaps the most powerful need that we have because when this need is not met, a person physically dies and doesn't have to worry about the other needs. A medical friend of mine has suggested that you only need six things to survive: food, air, water, sleep, removal of waste products from your body, and maintainence of your body temperature. It is interesting that a new born baby can only do three of these things for himself. He needs to have a caretaker provide his food and water, and help maintain his body temperature.

In the book of Genesis in the Bible is the story of Isaac and his twin sons, Esau and Jacob. Some people think that Esau was a dull boy because of some decisions he made in his life. He wasn't. He was raised by his father to be a prophet from the time he was little. He was his father's favorite. One day when Esau got very, very hungry and he sold his birthright--the right to be the prophet--to his brother Jacob for some pottage. It was a stupid act, but he knew what he was doing. He did it because he was very hungry. The need to stay alive is so powerful that people will do nearly anything to stay alive when the need is not met. They will do foolish things, illegal things (like steal), and sometimes even fatal things (eating polluted food).

However, there seems to be a time in the course of many people's lives when the spirit realizes it has accomplished all it can and no longer struggles to maintain life. It happens when people are old and have lived a good life. Younger people cannot understand it. Dylan Thomas is a good example. His father was dying and apparently was in the condition I have just described--willing to die. His father's attitude is disturbing to his son and so Dylan laments:

> Do not go gentle into that good night,
>
> Old age should burn and rage at close of day.
>
> Rage, rage against the dying of the light,
>
> Those wise men at their end know dark is right
>
> Because their words have forked no lightning.
>
> They do not go gentle into that good night......
>
> And you, my father, there on the sad height, curse.
>
> Bless me now with your fierce tears, I pray
>
> Do not go gentle into that good night.

Dylan thinks his father should struggle and try to stay alive. From Dylan's perspective, he would be struggling to maintain life.

Man does not live by bread alone, however. We have several other needs to care for. The following needs are just as powerful as the need to stay alive. When they are not met, the physical body does not die, but a person dies a little intellectually (senility), or spiritually, morally, or socially.

Children have a need to gain knowledge. It is to the spirit's advantage to learn things in this life. There is a Mormon scripture that puts it this way:

"Whatever principle of intelligence we attain unto in this life, it will rise with us in the resurrection. And if a person gains more knowledge and intelligence in this life through his diligence and obedience than another he will have so much the advantage in the world to come." (Doctrine & Covenants 130:18-19)

The nine months a fetus is in the womb is the dullest part of his whole existence. After nine months of this environment, the spirit is willing and anxious to be born. Doctors do not have to coax babies out of the womb. The spirit is probably thinking, "Get me out of here and let me have some 'hands on' experience!" The child wants to learn. Unfortunately a lot of parents unwittingly deprive their children of stimulation and the their children of stimulation and the chance to fill this need after they are born. They put their children in cribs or infant seats for the bulk of the day. An infant seat is a marvelous thing, but it pins the child's arms down to his side so he can't move. It also has a plastic protector that wraps around the side of the child's head. It is like blinders on a horse. It limits what a child can see. All he can do is look straight ahead. A child in an infant seat may sit for hours on the kitchen counter beside his mother as she does her chores for the day, and all he can do is look straight ahead at the side of a lime-green refrigerator. There is not a lot of stimulation in that. What happens to the spirit of a child who is stimulus deprived? The spirit gets restless.

When the child learns to crawl at six or seven months of age, the spirit says, "Go." And the child starts to explore. He gets into the pots and pans cupboard. He gets into his mother's purse. He gets into everything. This is not a bad child. This is a child with a healthy spirit. This is a child who wants to learn and who is making up for lost time. This small child is like the wolf in "Little Red Riding Hood." When he finds a new object, he fondles it with his hands ("the better to feel you with"), he may put it in his ear ("the better to hear you with"), or his mouth ("the better to taste you with"), or his nose ("the better to smell you with"), and so on. One of the author's daughters was thirteen months old at Thanksgiving one year. She was sitting in her high chair. On the table in front of her, within her reach, was a bowl of peas. She had never eaten real peas before. She got her hand on some of the peas and found she could roll them around on her high chair tray. Then she found that they fit up her nose. She started pushing peas up one of her nostrils as fast as she could go. Why do children do things like that? Why do they put things in their ears and nose, and bad tasting stuff in their mouths? It is a way to learn about the new object. Children use all five of their senses to learn about their world.

If a child is not having this need met, he will try to get someone's attention who can intervene on his behalf and fulfill this need. Many of you will have children who will struggle to fill this need. This struggle often happens in the midst of plenty--at school. In America, we believe in educating everyone. That is the democratic way. Many other countries do not educate everyone, but we try to. When you educate every child you have to use a curriculum that is at the level of the majority of children--the average child.

So public school curriculum is geared to the pace of three-time learners. But in classrooms there are one-time learners and five-time learners, and their needs will not be met with that curriculum. They are bored or lost, and they often resort to attention seeking behaviors to see if someone will give them a curriculum that will meet their needs. Teachers don't have time to reach the few very slow or very fast, and so parents have to pick up the slack and become active in educating their children.

Most fifth graders have spelling every day. They get a list of twenty-five new spelling words and practice these words at their desks on Monday and Tuesday. Then on Wednesday, they might, for example, have a pre-test to see how well they are doing. Then, on Thursday they might practice the words they missed on Wednesday. On Friday they could have the real test. In this arrangement, they practiced the words three times on Monday, Tuesday, and Thursday. What if the teacher told them that if the whole class scored a hundred on a spelling test, they could have a party. In most classes they would never have a party, because there will be at least two students that are five-time learners. They will never get it. They will just about get the words, but then it would be Monday of a new week, and they would get the new list of words to try and learn. There will also be one time-learner in this class. He or she will be so smart that they can read through the list of words on Monday and have them learned. He or she will want to do other things during spelling time the rest of the week but the teacher will say no. There will be three discipline problems in the fifth grade: the one-time learners and the five-time learners. One is bored and two are lost, but the problem is the same, even though it doesn't seem that way on the surface. The need to learn was not being met.

Children have a need to make order and sense out of their experiences. This need is expressed in many ways. It is one thing for a person to have a rich learning environment and learn new things, but it is quite another for him to make sense out of his experiences. But something inside of him propels him to try and do it. This need can be seen in very young children. When children are taken to adult activities, they do not understand what is going on. Their world becomes a world of nonsense. Small children struggle to make some sense out of what they are experiencing. Children twist things around until they make a little sense. You have all seen examples of this. It shows up in the funny little things that children say. For instance, "I pledge allegiance to the flag of the United States of America, ...one naked individual....with liver and tea for everybody." The words "nation indivisible" and "liberty" don't mean anything to a child, and so his mind twists them around into something that sounds familiar.

The lessons children learn as they are growing are not presented to them in an orderly fashion. Take, for instance, the television program "Sesame Street." In an average episode of "Sesame Street," there may be as many as thirty different, short, learning episodes. And few, if any of them, will be related. There may be a small section in which they will learn a number. A voice on the TV says aloud, "one, two, three, four, five, five, five, **FIVE**." This, accompanied by a picture of five Indians, and five bicycles, and five ice cream cones on the screen. Then that episode is over and four pictures will appear on the screen, three are alike and one is different and the child is asked to identify the different one. And then there may be a discussion of "near" and "far." None of the episodes are related. Sometimes at the end of Sesame Street, the producers will try and make it look like there was something cohesive about the program and so they will say, "The program today was brought to you today by the letters "B," "Y," "U," and the number 5.

Children have many small unrelated learning bursts and they don't know how to organize and make sense out of these experiences. It is a little bit like asking a person to put together a giant jigsaw puzzle without showing them the picture. It will be very difficult because while they have all the pieces, they don't know what to do with them. They don't know if they are putting together a flower garden or a horse race because each piece is so small that it doesn't make sense. It is the same way in life--someone has to help children see the big picture and help them fit each new experience into the total picture. Parents are that someone.

Children have a need to be in control of their lives. Everybody wants to make decisions in their lives and be in control. You can see this in very young children. If people don't get to make decisions, this bucket goes dry and they may resort to undesirable behavior. When parents with young children, ages 2, 3, or 4, insist on making every decision for them, such as what clothes they can wear, when they go to bed, and what they can eat, they are going to see some very negative behavior in their children. Their children may get very stubborn and resist others controlling them. They may fight back and rebel against their parents. Something inside of children makes them want to be in control of their lives by making choices. You can fill the bucket in little children by letting them make choices as simple as dressing themselves and feeding themselves. You cannot let children make all their decisions, however, because they are not wise enough.

The other side of this need is that when people get to make choices, then they have to be responsible for those choices. It is fashionable today to give children choices and then let them off the hook when they make a mistake. This is not a good idea. It teaches irresponsibility. It also demeans a child. Children almost always interpret such acts of mercy as a lack of confidence by the parent. Therapists and counselors tell us that when a family finally says to a child who has never had to be responsible, "We are going to make you be responsible for this act," it becomes the turning point in that child's life to getting back to "normal." This is sometimes called "tough love."

The guiding principle for parents who are trying to fill this need in their children is to ask themselves this question. "If I give my child a choice and he makes the wrong choice, am I willing to make him be responsible?" If a parent honestly doesn't think they can do that, they shouldn't give the child the choice in the first place. You do more damage letting a child make a choice and then not making them responsible for the choice, than you do by being dictatorial and not letting the child make a choice.

Children have a need to be close to others. This closeness can be filled in several settings--the closeness inside of families, and the closeness with friends. Families are the first social institution that children come in contact with. If a family is nurturant and takes care of an infant, she will feel like she belongs, and will bond to the family. The earliest bonding experience is close physical contact with caretakers. It is appropriate and desirable for a young child to be handled, cuddled, fondled, tweaked, tickled, hugged snuggled, and rubbed. Such physical contact bonds children to their caretakers. Humans never outgrow this need for close physical contact. By the way, this contact is not sexual in nature. People who try to fill the empty bucket for closeness through sexual contact, never fill the bucket. No matter how sexually active they are, their spirit never gets happy. That is why people are sexually promiscuous are never satisfied but are always searching for another conquest. They exploit people, but non-sexual physical closeness is very satisfying.

As children get older, there are other things parents can do to help them bond to the family. These activities involve sharing with a child. Sharing experiences with a child is good, but the greatest glue for bonding children to families is to share feelings with them. In today's hectic world this is hard to do because parents don't spend a lot of time with children, and so have very few opportunities to share feelings.

The emotions family members share don't have to be positive. In our society of mobile, nuclear families, the main shared emotional experience is usually grief at the death of a relative. When a death is unexpected or violent, the grief becomes more intense and its bonding potential increases. But, any strong emotion can bond people together.

Emotions don't have to be experienced together by parent and child. A parent can share an emotional event vicariously with his child. It is a good practice for parents to share with their children emotional events from their own past life.

Bonding cannot occur without spending time with the child. We hear the term today "quality time." Some people use this as an excuse for not spending time with their children. They say, "I'm not home much, but when I am, I'm really great." You cannot reduce the amount of time you spend with your child down to five minutes of red hot quality time. Not only do you have to have quality time but you also need to spend a lot of time with each child. A good guideline of how much time is at least fifteen minutes a day for each child, one on one.

Children realize that it is an act of love when parents share their resources with them. The more rare the resource that is shared, the more children perceive the sharing as being an act of love. They feel valued in their parent's eyes. In some families, the rarest resource will be money. If a poor family gave a child their last dollar, that would be seen as an act of love. But in middle class families, the giving of money is never seen as an act of love. Giving money may take away some guilt from a parent, but it is not an act of love. The rarest commodity in middle class families is time. Spending time with a parent is more precious than gold to a child. You have to give a child enough of your time so he recognizes that you have given him time--that you have shared with him. If a child does not feel a closeness to his family, he will seek for bonding in other places. The group he decides to bond with may not be a group you like. So you want to spend a lot of time bonding with your children.

==Children have a need to achieve.== Achievement means that a child wants to be special and outstanding in some way. A child can feel this by something as simple as having the best bug collection or being the best reader in a class. Middle class parents are pretty good at praising and encouraging their children, but the praise usually comes in only three areas of activity: academic activities (how well children are doing in school), athletic activities (are they on an athletic team), and cultural activities (can they tap dance and play the flute). If children take lessons in these areas, they will get better. So parents send their children to summer camps and give them lessons so that they get good at something. Excellence in any of those areas will certainly fill this need. A child that is a great student knows that they are a great student and they get a lot of satisfaction from that knowledge. If a child is a good athlete people let him know it. Unfortunately many children can not excel in any of these areas. They have talents in other areas. Such children are usually ignored by their parents and not given the opportunity to excel because their parents aren't aware of what to look for in the child. Some talents parents might look for are interpersonal in nature: leadership skills, compassion, ability to love, being a good listener, having empathy. Wouldn't it be amazing if some night at the dinner table a parent turned to a child and said, "You are the most loving child we have in the family and I just want you to know that we appreciate it?" The very idea sounds odd when you see it in print, but it is no more odd than when a parent talks about the grades or athletic accomplishments of children who are gifted in those areas. A parent should identify some areas in which their child can achieve and then give him the practice and praise so that he can be good. It is important to let older children in a family know of the talents of the younger children. It gives them status with their siblings.

Children have a need to share with others and to serve others. It is one thing to have a lot of talents, but it is another to move outside ourselves and share them. When people become totally egocentric and hoard their talents for use by themselves or a small group of friends, they wither away psychologically. Their bucket goes dry and they are not happy.

Humans need to serve and share with people. The sharing that works best is when other people do not know about it. It is not like when a group of friends divide up and pick a secret friend whom you do nice things for and at the end of the month reveal everyone's secret friend. In such situations children are more concerned about getting recognition for being the giver than the act of sharing. It is more like the Sub-for-Santa model in which volunteers do things anonymously. No Sub-for-Santa person would think about going back to a family in July and asking, "Did you like what you got for Christmas last year? We are the ones that gave it to you." Parents need to find opportunities for their children to do good work.

Children have a need to learn how to receive things. Isn't this interesting? We teach our children that they should be independent, stand on their own two feet, and not depend on anybody. We teach them that they are the masters of their own fates. But inside the child, the spirit knows that people have to live cooperatively, and that involves giving <u>and</u> taking. Most people don't know how to receive, and they feel uncomfortable doing it. There is nothing more boorish than a person who cannot receive a gift graciously. The Christian doctrine of the atonement teaches that people need to be humble and ask or beg for God's mercy. No person gains salvation on his own. He needs help.

A parent has to set the example of interdependence. We have heard angry parents say to their children, "I don't need you! <u>You</u> need me and don't you forget it." In a healthy family this would never happen. A parent should say, "I need you, I need this kind of thing from you and I recognize that you need some things from me." We need each other. Families should sing the song, "People, people who need people, are the luckiest people in the world..." once a week. We need to foster mutually dependent relationships. "No man is an island" John Donne once wrote.

Children need solitude. This means a time to be alone. A healthy person needs about 30 minutes a day to be psychologically and physically alone. During this time they can make plans, review the day, commune with nature, pray, write in a journal, or whatever. When people get so involved with their lives that they don't have that time, they will be neither healthy, nor happy. Sometimes students get themselves into such a fix. They take too many classes. Successful business people who are workaholics are not happy. They never have time to relax and think. Then this need is not filled. So they work even harder to accomplish more and feel satisfied. What they really need is to be less driven and more relaxed. Being over-programmed goes against the grain of the spirit. "What doth it profit a man" the scriptures say, "if a man gains the whole world and loses his own soul?" Some busy people don't even have time for the people they love.

Children have a need for beauty, and to be surrounded by beautiful things. Contrary to popular thought beauty is not always in the eye of the beholder. Beautiful things appear beautiful to many people. Many have seen beautiful buildings and paintings in life. Usually others have thought these were beautiful too. A healthy soul likes to be around beautiful things in music, art, and nature. A family should gather beautiful things and memories around them. There is something about putting money, time, and energy into making the surroundings that your children are growing up in attractive and beautiful. You do not have to be rich to have beautiful things. Being expensive and ornate does not necessarily make something beautiful.

Well, that is the basic list. It is not the exhaustive list. There are probably a few innate needs that we have not listed, but at the beginning we gave you the generic description so you could recognize any innate need. When you see the same need in every child, in every culture, and the need remains throughout a person's lifespan, you are probably looking at an innate need or need of the spirit.

The concept of the spirit is a powerful explanatory tool that helps us understand the human experience. It is the best and simplest explanation of why people act similarly. You will not find this discussion in any text book. But we are putting it in your reading.

PRINCIPLES OF DEVELOPMENT

There are several general principles of development that can help a person understand how children grow and how all systems work together. It is useful to study these principles at the beginning of a course because prevents repetition and gives a sense of unity to the study of children. When we understand that the same basic principles are influencing several areas of development, it appears children grow according to some grand design.

Principle one: <u>In those areas of development influenced by heredity, heredity sets the upper limits on what can be achieved.</u> Once our genetic potential is set at the moment of conception, there is nothing we can do to raise that potential. For instance, we all have a genetic potential for intelligence, and neither special instruction, nor diets, nor exercise can help a person raise that potential.

Principle two: <u>Learning waits for maturation.</u> This means that when you have a child practice to develop a skill, all the practice is wasted until the child is mature enough to benefit from the training. Research has shown that if you take identical twins, who have the same genetic potential, and give one of them practice in crawling up stairs from the time he is very young, and the other twin is given no practice, the second twin will crawl up stairs within a couple of days after the first twin has learned how. The reason for this is that all the practice with the first twin was useless until his brain and muscle system were mature enough to make use of it. Once he was mature enough, then the practice really paid off. When he was mature he learned very rapidly, and since his twin matured at the same time, when he was placed on the stairs he learned with just a few trials. Parents need to get a sense of their children's periods of maturation, to help them be realistic about what their children can accomplish. If a child isn't mature, then parents should relax and not push lessons on a child.

Principle three: <u>The environment acts as a drag upon potential.</u> While it is very difficult environmentally to raise somebody's genetic potential, there are many things that can lower that potential. In the case of intelligence, a high fever, some diseases, and injuries to the head can all lower the potential. Once the potential has been lowered, it is difficult or impossible to restore it.

Principle four: <u>Development is orderly</u>. While it may not seem so to a casual observer, there is a grand design on how children grow into adults. One of the orderly processes is called the cephalo-caudal principle. It states that a child grows from the head towards the foot. Another closely related principle is called the principle of proximo-distal development. This states that a child matures from the central part of his body (the spinal column) out towards the periphery (his toes and fingers).

In the chart below the bottom line represents an increase in age from birth to maturity and the vertical line represents how mature somebody is--immature at birth

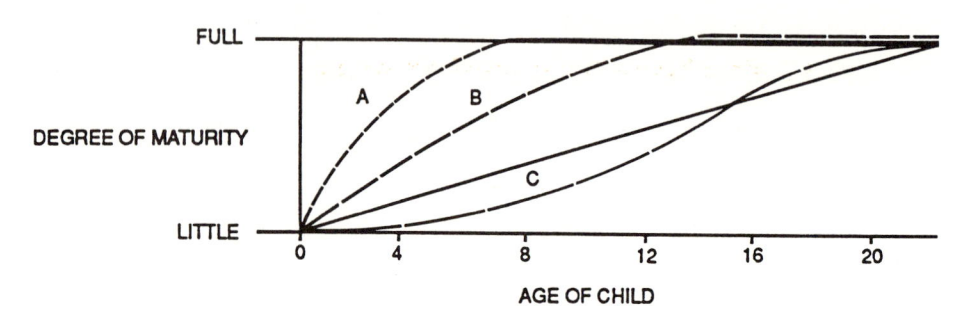

until fully mature as an adult. The straight line shown in the graph is a phenomena that <u>never</u> happens, so you can just cross it out. If it were a true phenomena it would mean that for every week, month, or year that a child lives, he increases the same amount in whatever area he is developing, e.g. two inches every year, five pounds every year, six IQ points every year, etc. There is nothing that operates this way.

Principle five: <u>While development is orderly in each system, there are periods of rapid and slower development</u>. The other curves in the graph show some of the typical ways that children grow. Notice that in curve 'A' the child is mostly mature by the time he's four and very little development takes place after that, while in curve 'C' very little development occurs for the first twelve or so years of life, then there is some rapid development, and within a period of two or three years the person is mature.

Principle six: <u>Different systems in a child follow different growth curves</u>. Not all systems experience periods of rapid growth at the same time.

Principle seven: <u>In normal, healthy children the sequence of development is always the same</u>. The timing of development can vary widely, but the sequence is the same. Hence

28

all children learn to sit up before they learn to crawl, they learn to crawl before they learn to walk, and they learn to walk before they learn to run and skip. But different children learn to walk at different ages and they spend different amounts of time in each stage.

Principle eight: <mark>In each of the systems which develop in a child, there are critical periods</mark>. A critical period is usually a time of rapid change or when the curve is the steepest in the chart. During critical periods a child is particularly susceptible to environmental influences for both good or bad, so parents should be vigilant of those critical periods in order to give children the proper guidance, to help them develop correctly, and to protect them, especially from harmful events that could throw them off track.

Principle nine: <mark>Children have a built-in catch-up system</mark>. If a child is not developing properly due to environmental factors such as illness, stress, or whatever, <u>and</u> the bad cause is eliminated, the child will develop faster than normal for a period until he makes up the developmental ground he lost. In other words, he catches up to what he was supposed to have been--remember that he cannot exceed it (principle one). In the diagram below the solid line represents how a child is programmed to develop, and the dotted line represents how he is actually developing. Notice that he is right on target

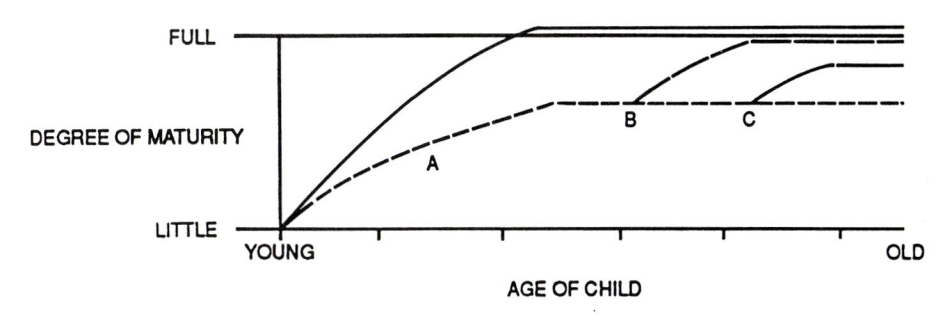

up to point 'A' and then something in the environment causes him to develop below his potential. If somebody intervenes in the environment between point 'A' and point 'B', and corrects the event that pulled the child off of his developmental curve, the child will grow faster than expected and get right back up to his potential. Such a time period exists in just about all phases of development. The length of time between point 'A' and point 'B' varies with each system and between people. If a person waits past point 'B' to intervene and intervenes between points 'B' and 'C,' there will be a partial catching up. The closer the intervention takes place to point 'B,' the more a child will catch up; the closer to point 'C,' the less. For some systems there is a point of no return. If you wait past point 'C' to intervene in a child's environment, no catching up will take place at all. For some systems in human development there is no point 'C.' It should be a source of comfort to prospective parents to know that when something interferes in a child's development and an alert parent becomes aware of it, they can do something that will help their child reach his full potential.

Principle ten: <u>All systems are coordinated in their development.</u> In the earlier graph notice that while some systems were growing fast, others were more or less dormant and then those roles were reversed. Apparently humans do not have enough energy to grow rapidly on all systems at the same time.

Principle eleven: <u>As children mature they go through certain stages when little progress is made</u>. There will be periods of rapid change and then a stable state or stage. Another time of change and another stable state. Sometimes the change is very dramatic and sometimes less so. Sometimes a stage lasts for a long time and sometimes for a short time. The chart below depicts what this looks like. Plateau 'A' is of average length, plateau 'B' is below average, plateau 'C' is even less, plateau 'D' even less, and

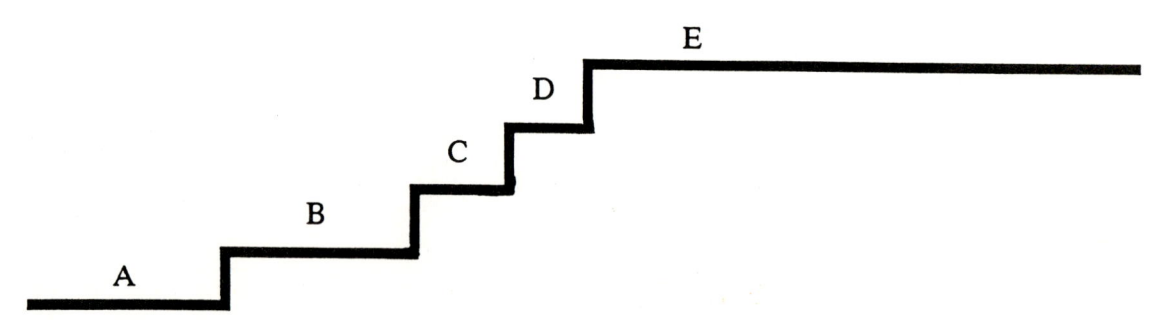

then plateau 'E' is very long. The change between 'A' and 'B' is of an average amount, between 'C' and 'D' is great, and between 'D' and 'E' is very little. The concept of stages is very useful and there are two insights that are associated with it. The first insight is that children always want to be a stage or two ahead of where they are. When children are preschoolers they want to go to school and when children are school age they want to do the things that adolescents do. Parents who don't know any better let their children get away with this, but a good parent will make a child stay in each stage until they have matured and accomplished what they need to do in each of those stages. This means that matured and accomplished what they need to do in each of those stages. This means that if a family has several children with a wide age range, the parent will be very busy organizing experiences that are appropriate to each age child. It is very difficult to have a meaningful family night with children that are both very young and very old because children of different stages have different kind of needs and experiences.

One way to visualize the stages of children is to picture that a child at each stage is like a different animal on the farm. Instead of the letters 'A,' 'B,' 'C,' 'D,' 'E,' on the chart, you could write "cow, pig, horse, chicken, goat." A farmer cannot go to the feed store and say, "I want a ton of chicken chow" and expect all the animals to like it. Each animal has a different kind of diet, different kind of exercise, and different things they need to be doing. That's what children are like.

The second insight is that farmers always have favorite animals. They may love all the animals the same, take care of all of them, and appreciate their value to the farm, but they have a favorite--and so do parents. It is just about impossible for a parent to be psychologically in tune with each different stage of childhood. Some parents relate well to infants. Others are soul-mates with school age children, and others get along excellently with adolescents. Often a child that is in a stage that a parent relates well to becomes the parent's favorite. Parents do not need to apologize for this. What they need to do is recognize it and then not <u>act</u> as if they had favorites. To have a favorite does not mean that you do not love, care for, and appreciate your other children.

Principle twelve: ==Children's minds always race ahead of their bodies==. Children can picture doing things that they are not physically capable of doing, e.g. a two year old wanting to ride a bike, which he is unable to do. Since this is a principle with adults as well, we can see it in our own lives. All of us can picture ourselves doing things--being great athletes for example--but our bodies won't respond. For a healthy adult a failure like this is not a devastating thing because we realize we have other strengths. But for a child who doesn't feel competent and who may not have high self-esteem, to dream a dream and then have it fail becomes very frustrating. A typical example would be a child who wants to draw a picture for his mother. He laboriously draws his picture and after spending many minutes on it, suddenly rips it up and throws it away. The reason he does this is because his mind can see what he wants to draw but his body won't do it. If parents are supportive of the art efforts and reward the process of him drawing instead of the product of the child, then his frustration will be less.

Principle thirteen: The process of development is more important than the product of development. In school a teacher might give the class an assignment to learn all about the state that the children live in, and grade the final paper on how much information they had, how neat the papers were, and so on. This is a product-oriented teacher. Alternatively, a teacher could realize that the most important thing was to teach a process of how to look up information, synthesize it, organize it, and present it. Such a teacher does not care much about the end result, but judges pupils on the kind of progress they are making. When parents have this attitude, they will never compare one child to another. As long as a child's foot is on the right developmental path and headed correctly, they know that the child will eventually reach the goal. They know that some children will go faster than others, so it does not become a concern. They compare the child to the child himself and not to other children.

Principle fourteen: The principle of correlation or, as someone once put it, "Them that has, gets!" It is the opposite of the principle of compensation which most people seem to believe. The law of compensation says that if a child is gifted in some area, such as intelligence, then they will be deficient in another area. You have heard statements like, "Beautiful, but dumb," or "Smart, but awkward." Compensation is not the true principle. The true principle is that those people who have received great genetic potential in one area seem to be above average in nearly every other area. The bad side of the coin is that the opposite is also true. When children are handicapped in some area, they are usually multi-handicapped. We speak of syndromes--whole clusters of things that go together. Good things go with good things; bad things go with bad things. However, no matter how handicapped children are, each has some area to excel. This is very hard for most psychologists to explain. The main character in the movie 'Rainman' is an example of this.

Principle fifteen: Children grow best in the shade. This is just a cute way of saying that children develop and flourish when they are in the shadow or shade of a parent or caretaker who loves and watches them, and is close enough to be aware of what is going on in their life.

Principle sixteen: Children seek for fulfillment.

Principle seventeen: Children can learn to cope with nearly any environment that is consistent.

LEARNING DISABILITY

In this day and age it is surprising that we are barely discovering enough about learning disabilities to be of effective help. Even the people who are closest to the problem generally are still not informed about screening or identifying children with LD. Therefore, many children are going through school feeling frustrated, being ridiculed and emotionally damaged because they think something is wrong with them. Something is wrong with children with learning disabilities, but it is not their fault. They are neither stupid nor deviant. They have a learning disability which makes traditional learning experiences more difficult and frustrating.

We used to think that learning disabilities were problems with the sensory system. So psychologists tested for visual, auditory, or motor deficits. Researchers finally demonstrated that learning disorders were cognitive, not sensory, and now our tests and procedures are designed to identify and help with cognitive problems. There are three types of learning disabilities: reading, math, and writing. Spelling is considered part of reading and every child with learning problems will have difficulty spelling.

In order for us to be effective in helping LD children, we need first to appreciate a few things. First, such children are not unintelligent or uncreative. In fact, a high percentage of LD children are both intelligent and very creative. Leonardo de Vinci and Thomas Edison are examples of intelligent and creative people who had learning disabilities. Second, LD children can be helped if parents and teachers can avoid emotional hysteria and practice effective and helpful measures. Third, LD children are different. They do not learn the same way, nor at the same rate as many other children. To some extent then they deserve adjustments made in their behalf. The problem, of course, is that teachers who teach large numbers of children and parents with more than one child often find it difficult to adjust enough without sacrificing other children's needs. This means that an LD child presents both a school and family problem. Therefore, parents should communicate with school personnel and vice versa.

Because most of us will be parents and others will be teachers, it is useful to become acquainted with the symptoms of learning disability. Doing so will enable us to be more informed and perhaps more helpful.

SYMPTOMS OF LEARNING DISABILITY

The primary reason it is important to correctly understand children with learning disabilities is to save them from further difficulty presented by uninformed parents and teachers. When children are not able to demonstrate success many assume incorrectly they are failing to apply themselves adequately or are malingering in some other way. Children with learning disabilities are different from children who learn normally, but they are not failures until or unless our inadequate understanding and treatment confuse and hurt them.

The following are common symptoms of learning disabled children. Few children will manifest all of them, but all learning disabled children will manifest at least one or more. Taken from The Learning Disabled Child, (Stevens, 1980).

1. **Mixed Dominance - Common**

    It is normal for children to do more things with one side of the body than the other. Mixed dominance exists when a child eats with his right hand, writes with his right hand, but draws and throws with his left. Some children do not establish cerebral dominance until the age of six or seven. Therefore if a child manifests mixed dominance after that age it is likely a symptom of learning disability.

2. **Directional Confusion - Typical**

    LD children frequently have difficulty with directions. They may be able to point to the north or south but cannot find the right word to use at the same time. They may confuse instructions to find something "over there" or turn right and you will see the house." In addition, they may be confused about right or left when asked to distinguish between ears, eyes, and hands.

3. **Similar Learning Problems in Other Family Members - Typical**

    LD children often have parents, uncles, or other family members who also have learning disabilities. There is no clear evidence that all learning disabilities are inherited but there is enough to suggest that at least thirty or forty percent of the time, other family members will also have disabilities.

4. **Extreme Difficulty with Sequencing - Typical**

The learning disabled have a very hard time remembering a series of things in order. At first this may not seem to be too much of a problem but it usually causes great difficulty. In this case the child will have difficulty remembering the alphabet, the months of the year, the digits in a phone number, or other numerical sequences.

5. **Slow or Delayed Speech Development - Not Common**

Some children are slow to develop in all areas. They may have speech difficulties and sometimes these may be a part of a learning disability. Usually, however, lags in speech development are just that: developmental lags that will be corrected with maturation.

6. **Difficulty with Time and Time Relationships - Typical**

This may manifest itself as difficulty reading a clock, or difficulty following time directions such as "be home by five." In addition, children may have difficulty using time to regulate themselves such as bed times, times allotted for chores, or mealtimes. Usually a signal has to be given to help a child recognize a certain "time" has arrived. Practically this may cause little problem because children rely on others for time. But to the child it may add further evidence of their stupidity and further confirm that something is terribly wrong.

7. **Retrieval Problems - Rare**

This usually appears as difficulty finding the right words to express in a given situation. Children with this problem will lose arguments, will not be able to discuss ideas well, and frequently be misunderstood. They may be able to take words in okay through reading and listening but they may have difficulty writing and speaking. So they often appear to be lazy, daydreaming, indifferent, or to have a mental block. If you notice that these behaviors are present when a child is faced with the task of expressing himself then a retrieval problem likely exists.

8. **Poor Motor Control - Common**

   This is manifest in clumsiness and awkwardness. These children will usually be the last chosen for a ball team and will show poor coordination at other times. They may be able to draw or write well but have difficulty in the larger motor tasks.

9. **Problems with Attention, Short Attention Span - Typical**

   The LD child tends to have an extremely short attention span. This means that he will tune into nothing briefly but just as quickly will go on to something else. his attention is demonstrated in short bursts.

10. **Distractibility - Typical**

    Most LD children are easily distracted. The least little noise or disturbance breaks their concentration. That is why they benefit from small school classes that are tightly structured to keep them on task and be effective in their work.

11. **Hyperactivity - Common**

    Besides short attention and distractibility, hyperactivity is a common indication of learning disability. In this case the problem is physical. A hyperactive child cannot sit still, is constantly in motion and will wander, bounce, wiggle - always on the move. Some learning disabled children are hyperactive, but most are not. Further, hyperactivity is not necessarily a learning disorder. So it is important to understand whether hyperactivity is part of a learning disability or not. It is a medical problem that can often be treated with appropriate medicine. However, it's treatment should usually involve psychological help.

12. **Tendency Toward Reversals - Typical**

    A learning disabled child will often read letters backwards and sometimes upside down. A child may look at the word "got" and read "pot," "dot," or "bot." Certain letters will be reversed more commonly than others. These are m, w, n, u, b, d, p, g, and q. This problem may also show up in math where a child will scramble the order of numbers such as making a 720 into a 270. All young children make reversals but most grow out of them. LD children do not and by the age of eight or nine distinctly show a tendency to reverse letters and sequence of numbers.

13. **Poor Oral Reading - Typical**

    This manifests itself usually as difficulty reading the small words. Some parents and teachers are confused because the same children who can read words like "elephant" and Mississippi" cannot easily read "who," "from," and "what." They may be intelligent in many other ways but have difficulty with oral reading all their lives.

14. **Poor Handwriting and Dysgraphia - Common**

    When first learning to write LD children have trouble remembering what the different letters look like. A child may know that he needs to make a letter "g" but instead makes a "y." Few children will manifest all writing problems, but all learning disabled children will manifest at least one or more.

15. **Inability to Copy - Common**

    This means that a child will have difficulty copying examples of other written words. This may include copying addresses, phone numbers, dates, and times. It is a frustrating problem.

16. **Poor Spelling - Typical**

    Difficulty with spelling is the most sensitive indicator of a learning disability. Many LD children conquer their problems in other areas but never manage to become better than adequate spellers. Almost all LD children are poor spellers. This is often caused by difficulty in remembering a sequence of letters and the tendency to make reversals. Also, LD children often do not have good visual memories.

17. **Trouble Getting Ideas onto Paper - Common**

    Even though a child may be good at expressing himself orally, if there is a learning disability a child may not be able to easily put these thoughts on paper. He will hate to write and may frequently complain, "I don't know what to write about." Such a child may also explode with frustration when faced with a writing task.

18. **Behavior Problems - Typical**

    It is frustrating to have a learning disability. Many LD children demonstrate this frustration by disobeying rules in school, at home, and with friends. They may also demonstrate emotional problems such as high anxiety or inability to adapt from one situation to another. They may occur because of the learning disability itself or because of late cognitive development and beliefs that they are stupid or otherwise flawed. Usually the lack of traditional success in school and elsewhere motivates them to find a place where they feel accepted and difficult tasks are not required. Unless treated properly, behavior problems can set the stage for future difficulty such as delinquency and criminal behavior.

19. **Creative - Common**

Learning disabled children are frequently very creative. This may be manifest by inventiveness of artistic creativity. Leonardo de Vinci and Thomas Edison are two famous examples of creative people who also demonstrated disabilities.

LEARNING ACTIVITY

Objective: To increase your awareness of and sensitivity to the manifestations of learning disability.

1. Rate yourself on the nineteen items identifying learning disabilities. Record those you do well and those you do with greatest difficulty.

   Those I do well   Those I do least well
   _____   _____
   _____   _____
   _____   _____
   _____   _____
   _____   _____
   _____   _____
   _____   _____

2. Make up a small survey and ask ten people to complete it. Ask questions that will help you determine how much people know about learning disability and how wide spread learning problems are among the ten people you survey. Show your questions and your results.

   _____
   _____
   _____
   _____
   _____
   _____
   _____
   _____
   _____

3. Develop a brief family strategy designed to help a child with learning disability. Consider such things as your method of discipline, where to find help, how to help siblings get along with an LD child, and how to encourage and provide emotional support.

   _____
   _____
   _____
   _____
   _____

PERCEPTION

Learning about the world begins with the processes of sensation and perception. Sensation is the process of having some nerve in the ear, or the nose, or the eye stimulated, which sends a message to the brain. Sensation is an anatomical function. Most parents will have no influence at all upon how a child senses the world. The only exceptions to this would be a child who is totally or partially blind or deaf. Parents of such children could help them gather information by providing them with hearing aids or glasses. But over ninety-five percent of the children are born with sensory equipment that works and they do not need any help to experience the world. So sensation consists of a stimulated nerve sending a message to the brain.

Dozens of impressions are sent to a person's brain every moment of their life. There are so many messages that the brain cannot notice all of them. The process of noticing a message that is coming to the brain is called perception. Parents have a great deal to do with helping a child perceive the world. Children do not know which of the many messages that are being sent to their brain they should notice. It is not the case that a child innately knows which messages are the most important. Someone has to teach him.

Figure 1 will look familiar to you. The line has two sections, A to B and B to C. Look at these and decide which of the two parts of the line is the longest. You've seen this many times so you know that line AB and line BC are the same, even though they don't look the same. But if you saw this for the first time, what would you think? As a matter of fact, since we knew that you have seen this many times, we have purposely made the line so that AB is longer than BC. You can measure it with a ruler if you want to. Illusions like this are tricks that our brain plays on us. Even as adults we don't always perceive things accurately.

FIGURE 1

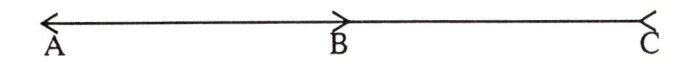

A third reason for inaccurate perceptions is that our past experiences influence how we interpret things. If three people see the same car wreck, they often give the police three different versions of what happened. The task of parents is to help a child perceive the world accurately.

There are seven things that a parent can do to help a child perceive the world accurately. First, if a child is going to perceive the world accurately, he has to be paying attention to the world around him. An old story is told about a farmer who owned a donkey and sold it to his neighbor. In a week the new owner came back to the seller and said, "You have cheated me, this is a very dumb donkey. He won't do a single thing." The original owner then picked up a large board and hit the donkey over the head and then gave the command to "go" and the donkey started to trot. He then said, "turn left, turn right" and the donkey obeyed perfectly. The original owner then said to the new owner, "see, you only have to get his attention."

Parents do not have the option of hitting their children on the heads with boards, but they can do many things that will psychologically wake them up so they will pay attention. If a lesson is important for a child to notice, you will want to make the lesson stand out. You can do this in several ways. You can make something stand out from other competing things by making it bigger, brighter, or more colorful. You can do this by having dull things happen before and after the important event. For instance if we were to teach our children about chastity, we would not do it on a day like Christmas. Christmas is the worst day to try to teach a child anything because too many other exciting things are competing for his attention. Pick out a very dull time when you want to teach your most important lessons if you want your child to pay attention.

A second thing you can do to help children perceive accurately is to give them a first hand experience with the phenomena you want them to notice. If you want them to learn about a dog, show a real dog. You want them to learn about airplanes, take them to an airport. This is the value of field trips. It moves a child into the real world where all of their senses will be used. They can see and feel and smell the event or object. If you can't give children a first hand experience then provide the best second hand experience available. None of your children will ever stand on the moon. So children are not going to have first hand experiences with the moon, but they can see pictures and photographs taken on the moon by those who were there. They can see rocks that have been gathered and brought back from the moon. Both of these experiences are better than looking at photographs of the moon taken by telescopes. So give the best first hand experience that you can.

Third, build in redundancy. Redundancy is a fancy word for repeated exposures to an object or concept. You give children many experiences with the thing that you really want them to learn. If you are trying to teach the concept of red, you show them many red things and label them. You hold up a pencil and say "red," you show them an apple and say "red," you show them a red dress and say "red," you show them a book and say "red." The more things that they associate with the sound "red," the easier and faster they'll gain the concept of what red is. Adults usually do not like redundancy and don't need it because we have had so many experiences that everything new relates to something we've already learned. We make mental connections and know a lot about the new experience. But a child is not like that--they need redundancy. If a parent and a child see something new together, the parent, who has a vast background of prior learning, doesn't need to spend a lot of time perceiving the new phenomena. But a child will.

Look at Figure 2. Our language is redundant. Notice an English word in which half of each letter is missing. You probably will not be able to read it.

FIGURE 2

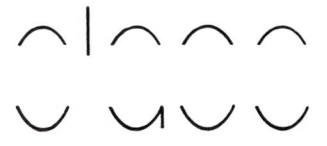

FIGURE 3

But, notice that Figure 3 has the same letters to which are added three small squiggles. Nearly all adults can read the word. Very few children at age five will be able to read the letters because they have not seen as many English letters as you have. English letters are so redundant to you that your brain fills in the missing parts.

Fourth, to help children perceive accurately, put new experiences into a framework of things they already know. Suppose you are taking a child on a trip and you are passing a goat farm. Take advantage of a teaching moment and say, "Oh look, out in the field. See the goats?" Your child looks out the car window and, sure enough, out in the field there are a bunch of goats--but there are also some cows, horses, pigs and chickens, tall trees and buildings, and a tractor or two.

The thing that catches your child's eye could easily become a goat for him. If he noticed a large tree, he might think that the tree is a goat. It's not enough just to point out something--you need to give the child a frame of reference. It would be nice if you would say, "The goat is an animal that looks like a large white dog." That's a pretty good description of a goat. As the child looks into the field he will eliminate cows and horses, pigs and chickens, trees, buildings, and tractors. In fact the only thing that the child could not eliminate would be a large white dog or maybe a sheep. When you make use of this principle, you should remember not to be too cute. Children do not have the same things stored in their minds that you do, and so the frame of reference has to fit the child's understanding, not yours. For instance, the parent in the car looking at the goats could say, "look at the goat! A goat is a mammal that looks like a miniature, cretinized, albino yak." This is a great description of a goat but none of the words have any meaning to a four year old, so he wouldn't know what you were talking about.

Lastly, when you teach a child something that you want him to store in his brain and be able to retrieve later, you need to give it a distinctive label. Suppose all the animals in the barnyard were called wig, wug, wog, woog, wag, wague, and so on. My heavens! The child would be seven before he knew the difference between a wug and a wog, and a woog and a weeg, and a wag and a wague! We give animals distinctive names like chicken, pig, cow, and horse, so a child can recognize them easily in his mind. By the way, the other side of this coin is that children innately "think" that when things have different names, they are different things. Makes sense, doesn't it?

Contemplate the confusion that arises in a three or four year old child, who has been taught that the name for his penis is "dingy" and who has three little friends who have been taught they have a "widdler," a "tweeter," and a "number one." These children are going to think that they are odd because no one else has what they have. To relieve this anxiety this little boy may sneak off and play games like "doctor & nurse" with his friends just to see how different he is from everybody else. What a relief when he discovers that everyone is the same (or at the most come in two varieties).

INDIVIDUAL DIFFERENCES

Most have at least an intellectual awareness that human beings differ from one another. We can see height, weight, skin color, and other obvious indications that this idea is true. Yet, at the same time we acknowledge we are different from one another we make general conclusions that certain groups of people are alike. For example, we might think, "all Idahoans or Californians or Chinese, or Americans are alike." With some prejudice we might even develop feelings of like or dislike about some groups of people and attempt to treat some groups of people with that attitude.

It seems more effective and mature to understand that humans are both similar and different. Moreso, however, understanding exactly how we are similar to and different from one another is a major part of all successful relationships. Parents, for example, are likely to be better if they recognize similarities and differences in their children. Then they can adapt what they do based on their knowledge of each child. Employers and supervisors are usually more effective if they understand each person as an individual. Likewise, husbands and wives have better marriages if they are able to communicate they can recognize unique characteristics in each other as well as communicate what they share in common. As we indicated earlier, all of these are possible if we can select a useful way to determine how human beings are similar and different.

SIMILARITIES AND DIFFERENCES IN CHILD DEVELOPMENT

First, let's recognize that there will be too many similarities and differences for all to be fully described. We can however, select some criteria or basis for you to use when you understand others. For example, young children demonstrate a set of characteristics called temperament which can be used to recognize both similarities and differences. Thomas and Chess (1970) compared and contrasted children on the basis of: (1) rhythmicity, (2) approach/withdrawal, (3) adaptability, (4) intensity of reaction, (5) quality of mood, (6) activity level. These six characteristics were used to determine similarities and differences in children. They concluded that EASY children are very regular, have a positive approach to others, are adaptable, have a low or mild reaction level, have positive moods, and demonstrate a variable activity level. SLOW-TO-WARM-UP children demonstrated varied rhythms, initially withdraw from others, adapt slowly, have mild reactions, have slightly negative moods, and have low to moderate activity levels. DIFFICULT CHILDREN are irregular in their emotional and behavior rhythms, withdraw from others, adapt slowly, have intense emotional reactions, negative moods, and varied activity levels.

Their scheme helped people understand how to compare infants and recognize similarities and differences. While this method may be very useful for infants, as children mature, we might be interested in using additional means to identify similarities and differences. For example, we might want to know about physical characteristics such as coordination, fine motor skills, and size. We might also want to know about cognitive style such as attentive or distracted, impulsive or reflective tendencies. Social maturity might include inclusion with friends or isolation. We might also compare and contrast children on the basis of emotional behavior such as expressive or inhibited. These are shown in the following table.

Physical Abilities	Coordinated	Awkward	Rhythmical
Cognitive Style	Attention/ Distracted	Impulsive	Reflective
Social Maturity	Included	Isolated	Disruptive
Emotional Maturity	Expressive	Inhibited	Volatile
Language Development	Verbal/Talks Nonverbal	Mostly Talks About Objects	Mostly Talks About People
Gender Characteristics	Masculine	Feminine	Mixed

When we are thinking about teenagers we might use additional ways to find similarities and differences. We might for example, be interested in early or late Physical development. Achievement behavior in terms of organization or disorganization. We might consider social behavior in the form of compliance or noncompliance, conversant or withdrawn, active or passive. We might also measure cognitive style, but in different ways

47

than we used earlier. For adolescents we might be interested in whether thoughts are abstract or concrete, integrated or fragmented.

UNDERSTANDING AND EVALUATING

At the same time we are learning about ourselves and others we acquire a system of evaluating what we learn. We start by thinking about it as good or bad, right or wrong. Later we might make comparisons such as better or worse, bigger or smaller. In any event these evaluations help us make judgments about what we do and how we act. However, many people mistakenly use a system of evaluation on other people before they take time to understand. Black or white skin, tall or short, thin or fat ordinarily are not traits which should be evaluated as good or bad, right or wrong. As part of improving your abilities to recognize similarities and differences in people, it will be useful to develop the skill of gathering information without making judgments about yourself and other people.

You can, for instance, learn to suspend judgment until you have had more opportunities to observe someone. In a conversation, for example, you might hear something and commit yourself to ask three more questions about a person's opinion before you allow yourself to evaluate it. You may also avoid evaluating someone when you know you do not have adequate amounts of information about them. Hearing a rumor (gossip) or watching someone in one situation is usually not enough information to make any kind of evaluation about someone and hope for any degree of accuracy.

Parents often make the mistake of evaluating before they understand. They establish rules which they expect children to comply with. When a child misbehaves, the strain of parenthood often results in impatience shown by instant scolding, spanking, or some other form of punishment. In doing this parents communicate it is their rule which is more important than the child. In contrast, suppose parents learned to talk, ask questions, until they collected enough information to make a judgment. Then, they may still discipline a child but the child will believe they have been understood and the discipline is related to the information given to the parents. In this way, parents communicate their ability to understand similarities and differences, or uniqueness, in each of their children.

LEARNING ACTIVITIES

Objective: To promote your understanding of similarities and differences in human behavior.

1. Organize a list of at least ten human traits (excepting physical or obvious characteristics). You might want to include traits from social, emotional, cognitive, or language categories.

2. Using these ten traits, make a questionnaire and collect information about four people by asking them to rate whether they possess any of the ten traits.

   EXAMPLE:
Trait	How Frequently do you Demonstrate
	Often Sometimes Never
1. Kind--	1 2 3 4 5

3. After gathering information, describe how all four individuals are alike and how they are different from one another.

4. Write a description of each person which includes information from the ten traits.

5. Select a friend or relative you see every day. Each day for five days ask this person four questions. In response summarize what you have heard without agreeing or disagreeing with anything he/she said. Then answer the following questions.
   a. Did the person tend to increase the amount he/she talked?
   b. How did you suspend judgment while you gathered information?
   c. which topics were hard and which were easy to avoid evaluating?

THE BRAIN AND THE NERVOUS SYSTEM IN CHILD DEVELOPMENT

During the last two decades neuroscientists have uncovered many hidden secrets about the human brain and nervous system. We now know more answers to many puzzling questions and also know there is much more to learn. The study of the brain and nervous system is at the forefront of science and offers many exciting discoveries in the years to come.

We are particularly interested in the brain as it pertains to other developmental concerns. We can assume that the brain is involved in everything humans do, but knowing how it is involved and how the brain accomplishes its purposes is essential if we hope to have a more complete understanding of child development.

THE BRAINS SMALLEST UNIT

Understanding the brain begins with some awareness of a motor neuron, the brain's smallest unit. Millions and millions of these cells are the tissue which form the structure of the brain and also determine how it functions. Each of these cells is made up of a cell body called a soma where the nucleus of the cells exists. The soma is like a message center which receives and sends electrical messages. It receives these messages from many fibers called dendrites. The message passes through the soma to one long fiber called an axon. An axon is coated by the myelin sheath, a fatty substance which insulates the axon fiber and increases the effectiveness of transmitting the electrical message. We can find axon terminals and terminal buttons at the end of the axon. These lie close to dendrites of other nerve cells and form synapses which are connections between neurons. The parts of the neuron can be seen in Table B1.

THE CENTRAL AND PERIPHERAL NERVOUS SYSTEMS

Cells such as those described above are organized into clusters and fibers. In every muscle and organ, these nerve cells are organized into two cooperating systems in order to

THE NERVOUS SYSTEM

Diagram B-1

To understand the nervous system and its functions, it is helpful to have some knowledge of its most basic units, the nerve cell or neuron. Although neurons vary in size and shape they have many features in common.

See diagram below.

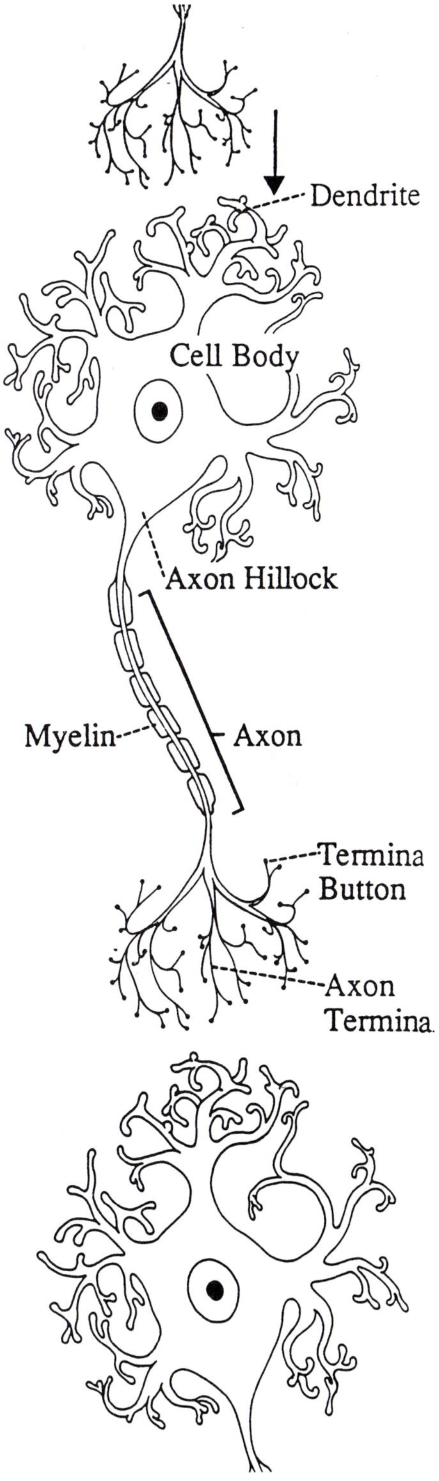

The Neuron

Axon: the fiber of a nerve cell (neuron) which carries nerve impulses away from the neuron cell body.

Axon hillock: the portion of the neuron where axon and cell body connect.

Axon terminal: (also called synapse) the junction between the axon end of one neuron and the dendrite or cell body of another neuron.

Cell body: another term is the soma. It is the portion of a nerve cell which includes a cytoplasmic mass and a nucleus, and from which the nerve fibers extend.

Dendrites: the nerve fiber that transmits impulses toward a neuron cell body.

Myelin: fatty material that forms a sheath-like covering around some neurons. Myelin is important with respect to the speed with which neurons conduct nerve impulses and with respect to the nutritional state of the neurons impulse conduction on myelinated fiber, which is ten to twenty times faster than conduction on unmyelinated fiber.

Terminal button or synaptic knob: tiny enlargement at the end of an axon that secrets a neurotransmitten substance.

51

collect information and transmit them to the brain and from the brain to other parts of the body. The nerve cells of brain and spinal column make up the <u>central nervous system</u>. The <u>peripheral nervous system</u> is a collection of nerve fibers lying outside the spinal cord in the skin and other organs of the body.

One part of the peripheral system is known as the autonomic division. It is divided into two parts, the parasympathetic-sympathetic divisions. The parasympathetic-sympathetic divisions are of special interest to us because this is the part of the brain and the nervous system that maintains a steady or homeostatic state. This normal or healthy feeling is maintained when arousal of the sympathetic system is balanced by the energy conserving efforts of the parasympathetic system. So, if there is great fear, sexual desire, curiosity, or other stimulation the sympathetic system responds but is balanced by the attempts of the parasympathetic to conserve energy. Both arousal and energy conservation seem automatic because they take place without conscious effort from us. (see diagram B-2).

THE STRUCTURE OF THE BRAIN

After learning a few ideas about the basic parts of the brain and nervous system, we can now go to reasons why the brain is fascinating. To begin with, our brains have several built-in abilities. That is, the structure of the brain is so organized that certain locations carry out specific assignments and these locations are organized in three levels. The BRAIN STEM consisting of the medulla, pons, midbrain, and diencephalon performs necessary but simpler tasks than the other, more superior parts of the brain. These tasks include the organization and management of simple and habitual muscle responses. The medulla contains sensory cells for the throat, neck, and mouth. It also integrates reflex activities such as control of respiratory and cardiovascular system. The pons contains nerves associated with sensory input and motor outflow to the face. The midbrain controls eye movement and the state of wakefulness of the entire brain. The diencephalon, a paired structure with a thin fluid space between the two parts (called the thalamus), is the major relay and integration center for all sensory systems except the sense of smell.

Diagram B-2   The peripheral nervous system can be subdivided into:

1. The **somatic division** which carries sensory information to the CNS from the skin and musculature.

AND

2. The **autonomic division** which includes those fibers that connect the CNS to visceral organs such as the heart, stomach, intestines, and various glands.

The **autonomic nervous system** is a portion of the nervous system that operates involuntarily, without conscious effort. It has specific functions and subdivisions:

A. Functions of the autonomic nervous system:
   1. Maintain homeostasis (equilibrium in the internal environment of the body).
   2. Regulate heart rate, blood pressure, breathing rate, and body temperature.
   3. Prepare body to meet demands of physical or emotional stress.

B. Divisions of automatic nervous system:
   1. The **sympathetic** division is concerned with preparing the body for energy-expending actions.
   2. The **parasympathetic** division tends to counterbalance the function of the sympathetic division in that they aid in restoring the body to a resting state following an emergency (see illustration).

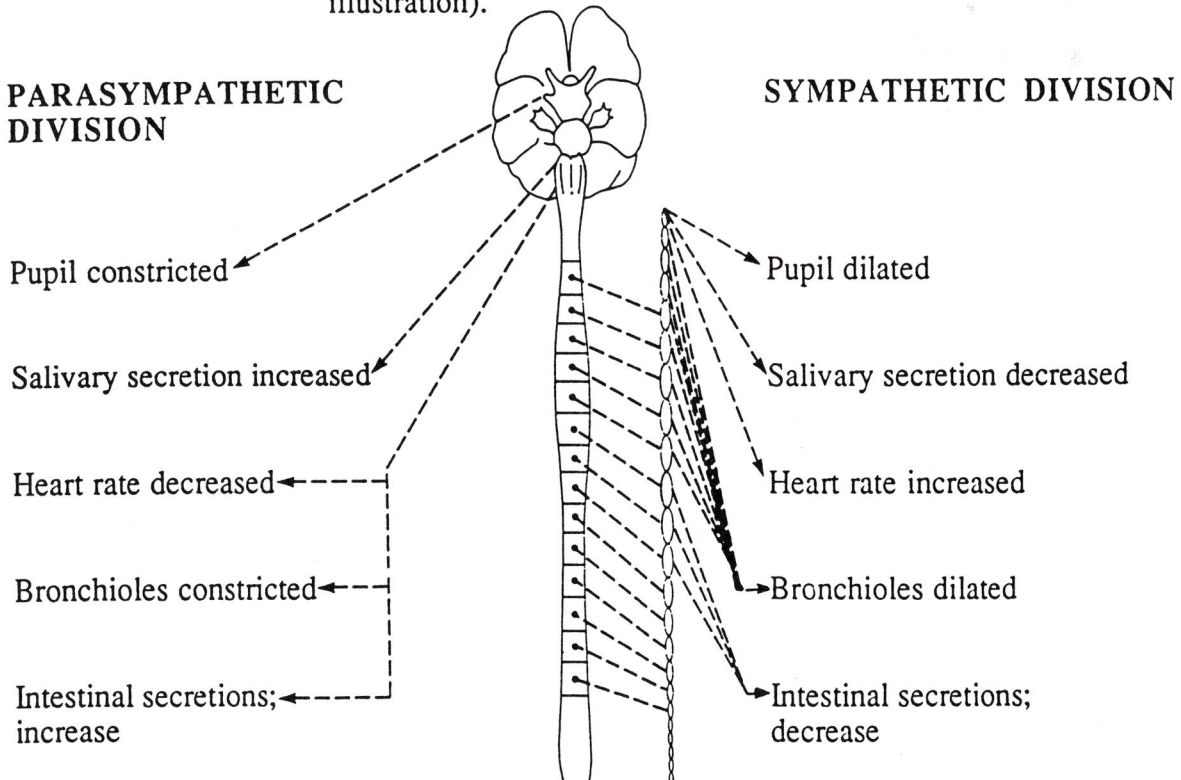

PARASYMPATHETIC DIVISION

Pupil constricted

Salivary secretion increased

Heart rate decreased

Bronchioles constricted

Intestinal secretions; increase

SYMPATHETIC DIVISION

Pupil dilated

Salivary secretion decreased

Heart rate increased

Bronchioles dilated

Intestinal secretions; decrease

The CEREBELLUM, located at the base and rear of the brain, is the center which controls the skeletal muscles in the trunk and limbs. All body movement is coordinated at this location.

By far, the most interesting part of the brain is the CEREBRUM or CEREBRAL CORTEX. Divided into two hemispheres and located at the top of the brain, this part controls the most complex human thought, emotion, and action. You should understand this is accomplished by how it organized. (See B3)

THE ACTIVITY OF THE BRAIN

First, consider the idea of LOCATION. This word has several meanings. It means, for example, that different parts of the cerebrum have specific tasks. In the left hemisphere, the locations for language and abstract thought are located. In the right hemisphere, the locations for understanding spatial relationships, ideational thought (visual images and simple language functions, see diagram B4) can be found. In addition to these locations, the cerebrum contains lobes or areas which perform vital, specific, and integrative functions (see B-5). As you look at diagram B-6, note that each lobe has a function as a sensory area and an association function with the rest of the brain.

In addition to hemispheric and lobe locations, there is another, even more complex function--of the cerebrum. Besides the idea of ascending or hierarchial organization, the cerebrum hunts for relationships between ideas. You can, for instance, be working on a problem and decide to think about something else. Your brain will keep working on a solution until one day you may have a pronounced "insight" because your cerebral cortex continued to work on the problem.

Lastly, in recent years we have heard about right brainedness and left brainedness. This pop psychology suggests that one person can use one hemisphere without the other. Rather, the brain works as an integrated unit. The two hemispheres are connected by a network of nerves known as the CORPUS CALLOSUM. This network enables the brain to communicate and also makes it work as a total unit. It is generally best to think of the brain as one wholly integrated unit.

DIAGRAM B-3

The Structures Composing the Central Core of the Brain

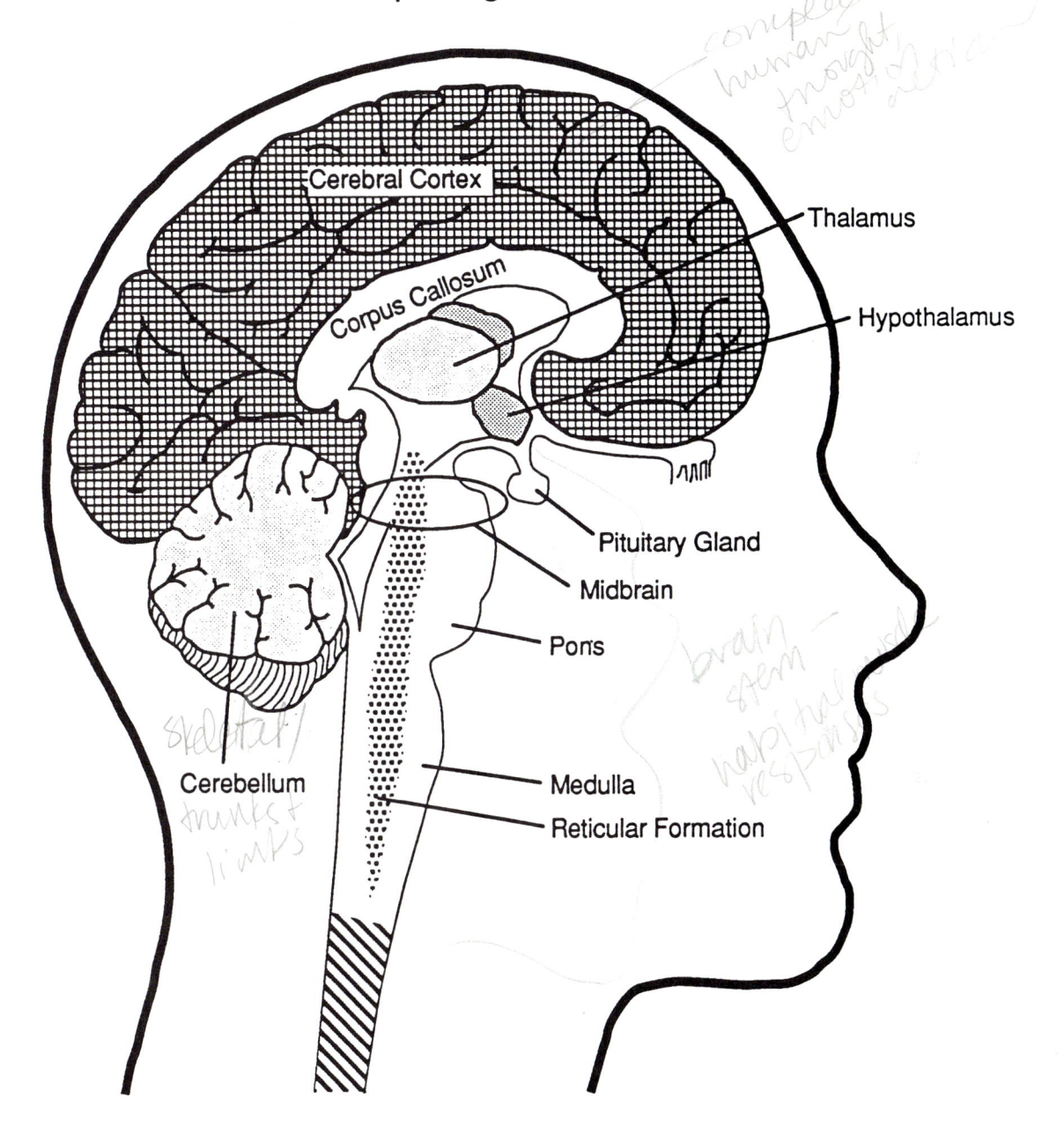

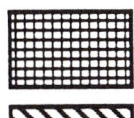

- Cerebral Cortex
- Thalamus
- Corpus Callosum
- Hypothalamus
- Pituitary Gland
- Midbrain
- Pons
- Cerebellum
- Medulla
- Reticular Formation

Most complex brain function

Least complex brain function

DIAGRAM B-4

Hemispheric Localization

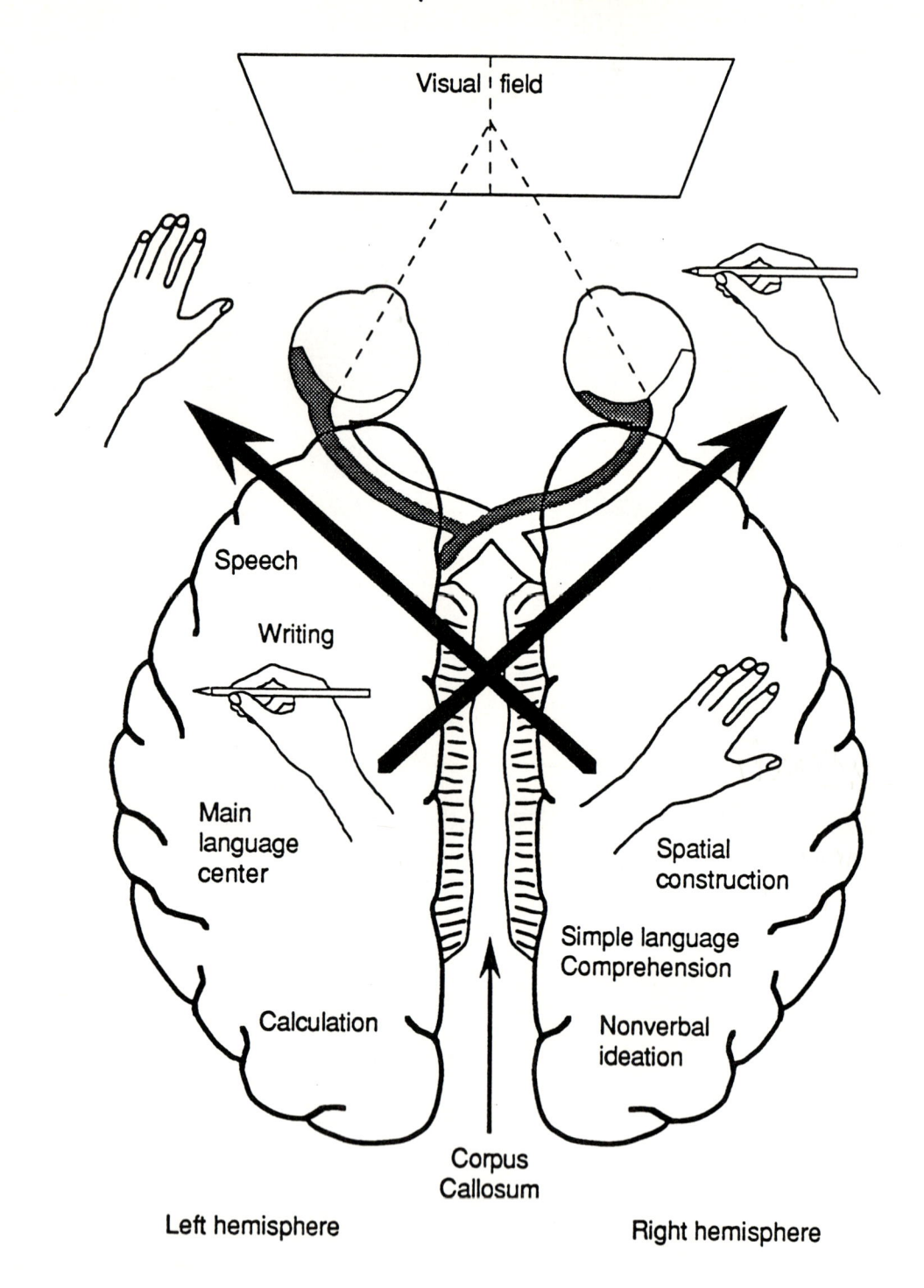

Visual field

Speech

Writing

Main language center

Calculation

Spatial construction

Simple language Comprehension

Nonverbal ideation

Corpus Callosum

Left hemisphere

Right hemisphere

Note: Males have more localized and specific functions than females

DIAGRAM B-5

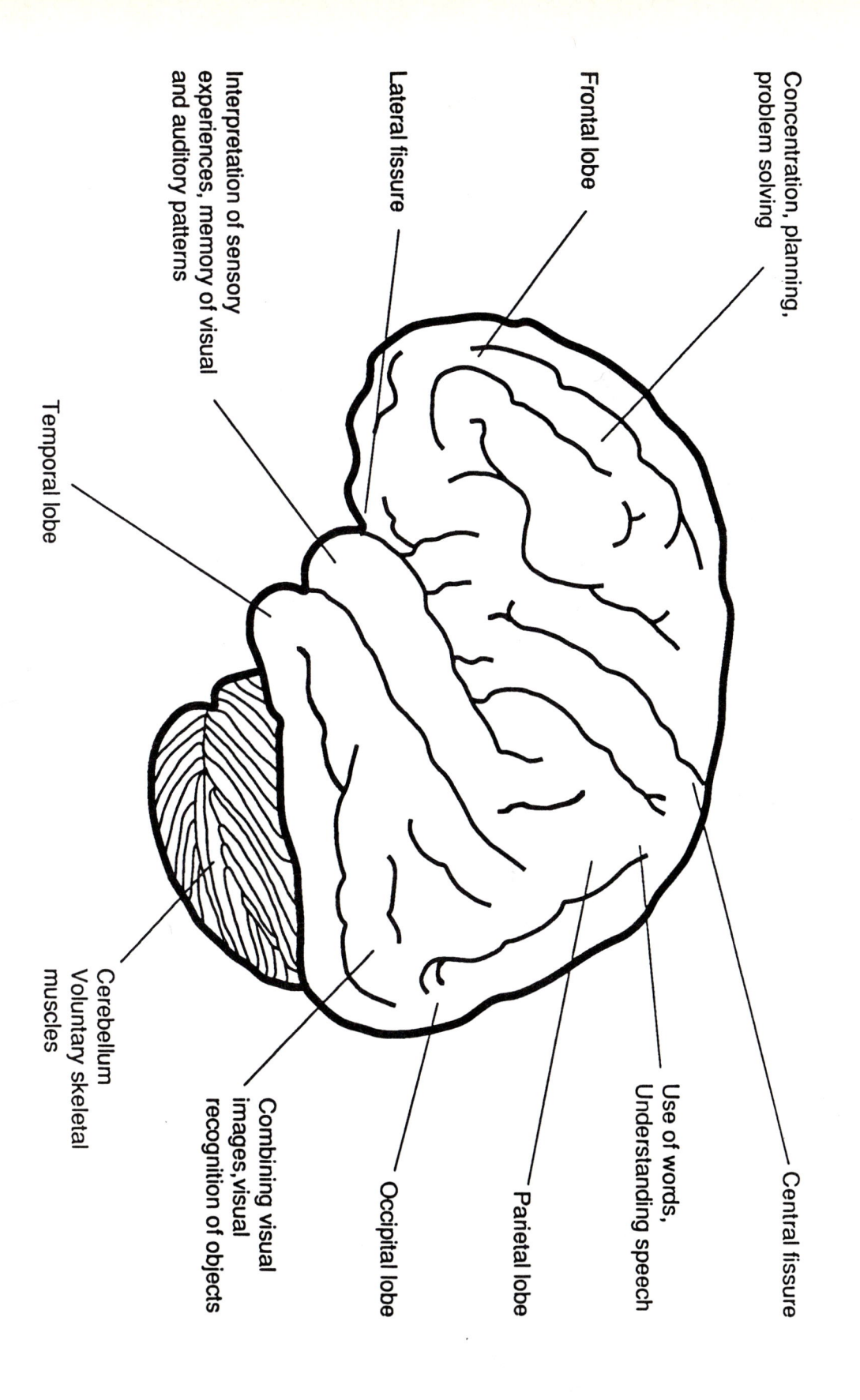

- Concentration, planning, problem solving
- Frontal lobe
- Lateral fissure
- Interpretation of sensory experiences, memory of visual and auditory patterns
- Temporal lobe
- Cerebellum Voluntary skeletal muscles
- Occipital lobe
- Combining visual images, visual recognition of objects
- Parietal lobe
- Use of words, Understanding speech
- Central fissure

DIAGRAM B-6

Frontal Lobes	Motor areas control movements of voluntary skeletal muscles.
	Association areas carry on higher intellectual process such as those required for concentration, planning, complex problem-solving, and judging the consequences of behavior.
Parietal Lobes	Sensory areas are responsible for the sensations of temperature, touch, pressure, and pain from the skin.
	Association areas function in understanding of speech and in using words to express thoughts and feelings.
Temporal Lobes	Sensory areas are responsible for hearing.
	Association areas are used in the interpretation of sensory experiences and in the memory of visual scenes, music, and other complex sensory patterns.
Occipital Lobes	Sensory areas are responsible for vision.
	Association areas function in combining visual images with other sensory experiences.

THE BRAIN IN CHILD DEVELOPMENT

Like other forms of development, the brain develops too. It begins as a cluster of cells on the caudal end of the embryonic disk. From that point on, if growth is unaffected by some teratogenic agent, the brain stem develops followed by the core (and cerebellum) and lastly the cerebral cortex. During the last trimester of prenatal development there is rapid development of brain cells so that at birth there are thirty to forty percent more brain cells than will be actually used. Most of these eventually die. After birth, brain development takes two forms. One is the creation of innumerable connections between the brain cells and the other is called myelinization. From birth through puberty, new connections between neurons are established. This development increases the efficiency of the brain and gives it increased capability. Myelinization refers to the growth of a fatty insulation surrounding the nerve axon. At birth this is incomplete and increases as an individual matures. This too enables the brain to work more efficiently. Brain physiologists suggest that intelligence or other cognitive skills such as memory, are probably a function of the number of connections and how fully myelinized brain cells are. The more connections, the more intelligent, etc.

Besides these physical developments, the brain develops according to the amount of stimulation it receives. If a child or adult adds great stimulation, the brain will respond by organizing cell structures to respond. Evidence exists, for example, that mental stimulation enhances natural maturational processes and retards the process of aging. This suggests to us that the wonderfully complex natural brain can be affected by how we treat it to some degree. The more stimulation we provide it, the more it will develop and the slower it will age. What will you choose to do?

LEARNING ACTIVITIES

I. Answer the following questions:
   A. What does the term LOCATION refer to?
   B. List the primary and association function of each cerebral lobe.
      1. frontal_____
      _____
      _____

      2. temporal_____
      _____

      3. parietal_____
      _____

      4. occipital_____
      _____

   C. What is the combined function of the sympathetic-parasympathetic division of the autonomic nervous system._____
   _____

   D. Describe how the brain develops from birth to adulthood._____
   _____
   _____
   _____
   _____

II. Describe the functions of the following parts of the brain structure:
   a. reticular formation_____
   _____

   b. neuron_____
   _____

   c. corpus callosum_____
   _____

   d. hypothalamus_____
   _____

   e. cerebral cortex_____
   _____

  f. limbic system_____
    _____
    _____

  g. cerebellum_____
    _____
    _____

III. Name the mental abilities found in the hemispheres of the cerebral cortex.
  a. Left hemisphere_____
    _____
    _____
    _____
    _____

  b. Right hemisphere_____
    _____
    _____
    _____
    _____

DETERMINE WHICH SIDE OF YOUR BRAIN IS DOMINANT

This is not a test to determine your intelligence. It merely establishes your style of thinking and learning. Put an X in the appropriate column, A, B, or C next to the description that is most like you. Mark only one X for each question. To find your score, turn to page 172.

	A	B	C
1. I remember best...	step-by-step pictures	descriptions of techniques	both
2. I prefer to have things explained to me...	with words	by showing them to me	both ways
3. I prefer classes...	Where I work on many things at once	outlining one assignment at a time	both
4. I prefer classes that...	allow me to choose between one or two projects	allow me to do anything I want	both
5. I prefer...	to decide for myself	to have others tell me what looks good on me	half and half
6. I think reading...	is working not fun	is fun	is sometimes
7. I prefer classes...	in which I can experiment	where I can listen to experts	both
8. I construct things...	by looking at directions	based on my experience	both ways
9. I tend to solve problems...	with a "maybe this will work" approach	with a serious business approach	both approaches
10. I like to use...	proper materials to get the job done	whatever is available	a little of both
11. I like my classes...	to teach techniques I can use on the problems at hand	to teach techniques I can use in the future	both
12. I am...	never inventive	very inventive	sometimes inventive
13. I prefer classes...	open with opportunities for change	planned so I know exactly what to do	both ways
14. I...	would rather not experiment	like to experiment	sometimes experiment
15. When doing a project like sewing, I like to...	change things to suit my tastes	add nothing to the original design or pattern	both ways
16. I get insights	rarely	usually	sometimes
17. I prefer...	solving more than one problem at a time	solving one problem at a time	both equally

	A	B	C
18. I respond more to a teacher when...	s/he appeals to my logical side, my intellect	he appeals to my creative side	both equally
19. I prefer to learn...	the unclear parts, the hidden possibilities	the well established parts of a subject	both ways
20. I prefer...	taking techniques apart and thinking about them separately	putting a lot of techniques together to do something creative	both
21. I prefer...	to use "gut feelings" in solving problems	to use logic in solving problems	both equally
22. I prefer...	to analyze problems by reading and listening to experts	to see and imagine things when I solve problems	to do both
23. I'm very good at things like...	machine embroidery, or free hand sketching...	sewing perfectly straight seams, or precise drafting plans	both
24. I learn best from teachers who...	explain with words	explain with movements and actions	have no preference
25. When I remember or think about things, I do so best with...	pictures and images	words	both equally well
26. I prefer to...	examine something that is finished and complete	organize and complete something that is unfinished	do both
27. I enjoy showing someone how to make something by...	drawing and manipulating (handling) things	talking and writing	both equally
28. I can...	follow written directions easily	follow verbal directions easily	both equally
29. I use...	intuitive approach	an intellectual approach	both equally
30. I prefer to learn...	details and specific facts	from a general overview	both ways equally
31. I read magazine articles...	for main ideas	for specific details and facts	for both equally
32. I learn and remember...	only those things specifically studied	details and facts not specifically studied	noticed no difference in these areas
33. I like to choose...	whatever is in style in each season	realistic classic clothing	no preference
34. I feel it is more to...	plan realistically	dream	both equally fun

	A	B	C
35. I...	prefer music while doing homework	prefer total quiet when doing homework	I listen to music only when reading for enjoyment, not when learning intricate principles
36. I would like to write...	for a technical manual	for a popular magazine	no preference
37. If seeking a workshop I would prefer...	group counseling and sharing or ideas with others	the confidentiality of individual counseling	no preference for group over individual counseling
38. I enjoy...	copying and filling in details	drawing my own images and ideas	both equally
39. It is more exciting...	to invent something	to improve something	both are exciting
40. I prefer to learn...	by examining	by exploring	both ways equally
41. I prefer...	sewing crafts	sewing clothing	both equally
42. I am skilled in...	putting something together one step at a time as directed	putting it together as I think it should go	both equally
43. I prefer...	buying something frivolous	buying classic, practical	both equally
44. I...	use time to organize myself and my personal activities	have difficulty in pacing my activities to time limits	pace personal activity and time limits easily
45. I jump from one project to another...	frequently	never	almost never
46. I am...	almost never absent minded	frequently somewhat absent minded	occasionally absent-minded
47. I am strong...	in recalling spatial materials	in recalling verbal materials	equally strong in both ways
48. I am skilled in...	the statistical, scientific prediction of outcomes	the intuitive prediction of outcomes	equally skilled in both
49. I prefer...	summarizing over outlining	outlining over summarizing	have no real preference
50. I prefer...	verbal instructions	demonstrations	no real preference

MORAL CONDUCT

It is easier to teach children to think about something than to help them know what to do, when to do it, and how it can or should be done. When it comes to morality, for instance, we typically want them to do what is moral not just think about it. As teachers, parents, and caretakers we are in a position to help children learn to do what is moral if we are aware and skillful in what we do.

First, we need a definition of morality that makes sense, is easy to teach, and will have power to affect children. Morality is simply the intent and/or acts which help someone and immorality is the intent and/or acts which harm someone. When we think about helping or hurting people it seems easy to reason about what will or will not help. Unfortunately, we often fail to teach children what helps or hurts people because we mistakenly think morality is related to conformity to rules. Those who have this notion assume that a child who complies with a rule or law is moral but this is true only if the law and obedience to it helps rather than harms human beings. So instead of thinking morality to be conformity or obedience, we need to teach ourselves and our children what helps or hurts people.

Coincidentally, teaching children about helping or hurting people is one of the most effective ways to ensure they will act morally when a time of moral decision confronts them. Think about a high school student who has had difficulty with a math teacher. This teacher is generally so disliked that many students have negative feelings. One day this boy is with a group of friends in the school parking lot. They notice the teacher's car and someone suggests letting the air out of the tires. Another says, "yeah, let's do it," as he moves closer to the car. Our friend is now faced with a moral dilemma. Should he let the air out of the teacher's tires or not? What will influence what he does? Suppose he says, "I don't know guys, we would be breaking a rule." Would that be persuasive to the other guys who might think, "what rule?" or "It's a little rule," or "it's stupid." Contrast that with the idea that letting the air out of someone's tires would be harmful to him. If the boy thinks about that, then he also might be able to put himself into the situation of someone who comes out of school to drive home and discovers that the air is out of all four tires. Would that line of reasoning be persuasive? Generally, the answer is that thinking about what helps or harms people is more directly related to moral behavior than pressure to comply with any rule.

What then does this have to do with getting children to do, not just think about, the moral thing? It focuses them on what they are to actually do. They are to help and not hurt themselves or other people. In addition, when we think about morality in this way it directs us to what we must do as teachers, parents, and caretakers in order to get children to act morally. Notice, for instance, how children who act morally differ from those who do not.

Children who act morally are more likely to have empathy for others which means they understand what others may think or feel. In contrast, children at higher risk for immoral behavior are defensive which means they are more likely to shift the responsibility for their actions to others and be unable to know about and discuss their own feelings. As a result they do not know what others feel because they do not know their own feelings. Moral children also tend to be more accepting of others or willing to understand other people without making premature judgments about them. Prejudice, judging people without gathering individual information about them, is often a characteristic of people who do immoral things.

One interesting condition which relates to whether children do moral or immoral acts is the amount of conversation they have with adults such as parents and teachers. If they participate more frequently in conversation relationships and are less isolated from others, they are more likely to make moral choices and act morally.

The following list are characteristics of those who are likely to do moral and immoral acts.

Moral	vs.	Immoral
Empathy		Defensiveness
Acceptance		Prejudice
Autonomy		Vulnerability
Social Interaction (Conversation)		Social Isolation
Activity		Passivity
Positive Moods		Negative Moods

A TEACHING PLAN

In light of the foregoing it is clear to us that we can influence children by helping them develop some character traits which they express in many different situations. In addition, there are some specific things we can do to ensure that children will do what is moral when they are faced with pressure to do otherwise.

Repetition:

This means that our focus on moral traits must be repeated so that children learn they are important to develop.

Rule Governed Behavior:

Children understand that rules exist for most situations. We can help them identify the rules for friendship, social activities, church, meal time, etc. However, we must also teach that rules or laws can help and harm people.

Internalize:

After children learn intellectually about helping and harming people, they must actually practice these traits and discuss them so they can test the ideas against their own experience. Later when they more clearly understand they are free to choose themselves, they will internalize these experiences, they will be moral people rather than merely thinking about doing what is correct.

LEARNING ACTIVITIES

Objective: To identify what behavior helps and harms people and the traits of moral people.

1. Identify and define four traits manifest in the behavior of moral people. What is the opposite of these traits? Explain how they harm people.

    Moral Traits
    a._____
    b._____
    c._____
    d._____

    Opposite of Moral Traits and how they harm people.
    a._____
    b._____
    c._____
    d._____

2. Describe a personal experience where you hurt someone or when you were harmed by someone. After describing the experience identify what happened to produce the harmful effects.

    _____
    _____
    _____
    _____
    _____
    _____

3. Ask four people to define morality. Write their definitions. Evaluate whether they think morality is
    (a) compliance with rules; and/or
    (b) related to helping or harming people.

    a. _____
    b. _____
    c. _____

4. Write a 3 page paper which describes how morality develops over time. Include a specific set of steps where children learn to help and not hurt.

FRIENDSHIP

Friends are an important source of influence on developing children. It is by association with friends that children are motivated to learn social skills, and friends give social reinforcement that provides emotional satisfaction. Friendship has received much attention from many writers. One wrote:

> A blessed thing it is for any man or woman to have a friend; one human soul whom we can trust utterly; who knows the best and the worst of us, and who loves us in spite of all our faults; who will speak the honest truth to us, while the world flatters us to our face, and laughs behind our back; who will give us counsel and reproof in the day of prosperity and self-conceit; but who, again, will comfort and encourage us in the day of difficulty and sorrow, when the world leaves us alone to fight our battle even as we can.
> --Charles Kingsley

Developmental psychologists have learned that children notice and are affected by other children from the time they are infants. Vandell, Wilson, and Buchanan (1980) reported that pairs of children aged 6 months, 9 months, and 1 year smiled, touched, and babbled to each other. When babies had no toys, they spent more time interacting.

As children develop, their behavior becomes more elaborate involving new social skills. Observations of preschoolers show that children who smiled and were friendly received more pleasant responses than children who pushed, shoved, or were mean in other ways. This suggests that children engage in reciprocal behavior at an age earlier than researchers thought possible. The children, however, were not aware they were doing so.

In later childhood, friendship develops into more elaborate forms of reciprocal behavior. They view sharing with each other as a sign of friendship and learn ways to give and receive. Some of these include material goods, compliments, patience with and acceptance of one another's mistakes, and helping each other with chores or work.

Eventually, friendship develops into a significant emotional bond where children share feelings and understand personality traits of one another. Adolescents select friends on the basis of companionship experience and similarity of interests.

From Leitner's study we might conclude that children naturally tend to be social and be friends one with another. Social isolation, therefore, must be the result of unfavorable social experience. Further, not having a friend or not having the skills to be one may interfere with the normal course of development.

Children will learn friendship behavior both as part of maturation and social learning. The biological aspect can be helped when children see positive friendship behavior, and when they have social opportunities themselves. Such social experience can be frequent and it can be varied. Parents often worry if their children are friends with children who are older or much younger. The evidence seems to suggest that conditions will not be destructive as long as the friendships are positive and have some meaning for children. The situation creating the most difficulty of course, is the absence of sibling friends or other good friendship experiences.

SEQUENCE OF DEVELOPMENT

<u>Stages of Development</u>

<u>Stage I</u> Momentary Playmateship 0-3	Before the age of four, children choose friends on the basis of some physical attribute or neat toy. Friendships last as long as children are curious and stimulated by the novelty or prestige of their friend's characteristic or possession.
<u>Stage II</u> One Way Assistance 4-9	Children enter this stage of friendship at the time they understand the intentions of other children's actions. Children are still selfishly interested in getting what they want from their friends.
<u>Stage III</u> Two-Way Fair-Cooperation 6-12	There is considerable overlap between stage 2 and stage 3. As children move into stage 3 their friendship styles weather change. They recognize that friendships require give and take, but in a way to satisfy self-interests. True concern for their mutual interests is not yet evident.

<u>Stage IV</u>
Mutually-
Intimate Shared
Friendships
9-15

Children form valued friendships. They are often exclusive, with children feeling quite possessive about them. Cliques of friends often form, excluding those not "in" the group. Emphasis is on loyalty to one another and mutual help giving.

<u>Stage V</u>
Autonomous
Interdependence
13-

Friendships have a deep emotional commitment. Children can understand the dependence on others and the need for autonomy. Concepts like trust, and risking caring for another are relevant. These friendships become life long.

LEARNING ACTIVITIES

I. <u>Reciprocal Giving</u>

   Objective: To show that reciprocal social exchanges are part of friendship skills.

   A. Do the following and record the number of responses you receive.
      1. Smile and say "hello" to ten different people.
      2. Perform ten acts of courtesy (opening doors, letting someone go ahead in line).
      3. Give ten small articles to other people (e.g. a piece of gum, candy, etc.)
      4. Offer to do helpful things ten times.
      5. Say ten complimentary things about your friends to other people.
      6. Compliment your friends 5-10 times.
      7. Tell some incident from your past to at least 4 different people.

   B. Report the frequency of response for each of the seven friendship behaviors. Which created the least? Which was the most comfortable for you to do?
      _____
      _____
      _____
      _____
      _____

II. <u>Friendship Styles</u>

   Objective: To show the influence of social customs on friendship behavior.

   A. Interview four people (two female, and two male). Ask them the following questions. Record their answers.

Two people have known each other for less than one day and spent less than two hours together. Determine which of the following would be acceptable to you.

Unacceptable   Acceptable

1. Tell a personal experience about something you feel guilty about.
2. Use each other's nicknames.
3. Inquire about details of one's background
4. Ask what work a person does.
5. Touch each other in affection.

6. Talk about politics.
7. Talk about the weather.
8. Give a complement about the way a someone is dressed.
9. Invite them to a future meeting.
10. Be critical of some prominent person.

B. Answer the following questions:
1. Describe the amount of agreement obtained from the four people.

2. Were the females in agreement with each other more than they were with the males?

3. What conclusions would you form from the results?

EMOTIONS IN CHILDREN

Our every day experience with emotions is so common we often do not give much thought to the role they have in our lives. Even if we recognize their importance, we often do not know what to do about them. This article is designed to help you understand the role emotions have in the lives of developing children.

Knowing the meaning of a few terms will help. EMOTIONAL STATE refers to physiological reactions of the body such as dilated pupils, heart rate, respiration rate, muscle tightening, etc. Love, for example, is associated with the heart because muscles close to the heart tighten in correspondence with that emotion. EMOTIONAL DISPLAY or expression refers to the many ways we express outwardly what we feel inwardly. Emotions may be expressed or displayed on our face, voice, posture, movement, and language style. EMOTIONAL EXPERIENCE is the subjective part of emotion. When you talk about your "feelings" you are disclosing your emotional experience.

HOW WE ACQUIRE EMOTIONS

Interestingly, researchers are still not certain about whether we inherit some emotions and learn others, or whether we learn them all or inherit them all. At this point in time, however, most are leaning toward the idea that some emotions are built into the structure of the brain. Therefore, some emotions like anger, anxiety, disgust, surprise and sadness are considered part of everyone's life. Other emotions such as love, for example, may be learned. To further support this idea, researchers point to the finding that fear is not apparent in most infants until about six months of age. For us, however, it is not as important to distinguish between inherited and learned emotions as it is to recognize that emotions are present early in life and play a major role thereafter. We do understand that emotions can be learned and children can learn a greater or smaller variety of emotions depending on the opportunities to do so. Further, we can learn more ways to display any emotion if we choose to do that. Lastly, we can for ourselves and for our children, develop or learn new ways to regulate the intensity of our emotional display. We can also learn to adapt our emotions to fit into increased numbers of situations.

EMOTIONAL MATURITY

About this point you might be asking why we should learn more emotions, more ways to express the same emotions, more ways to regulate them, and more ways to adapt them to different circumstances. This process is the pathway to emotional maturity. Children tend to manifest emotions without being aware they do so. They then acquire some awareness that different emotional states and experiences have their own name and accompanying display. That is, a person can discover anger and then he or she can display anger in certain ways. While this is taking place children also learn about more emotions, more ways to display them and also how to regulate and adapt them. For example, a child can be excited and talkative before going to church, but when in church needs to adapt or change the excitement to reverence. When a child cannot do that, we understand him or her to be less mature than one who can make these adjustments. Further, when children do not know how to regulate their emotional display this will be manifest in such behavior as temper tantrums, insecurity, withdrawal, bullying, aggressiveness, whining, and pouting. These characteristics, of course, are usually associated with the less mature.

When parents are faced with immature displays of emotions, they try to help children assume control over their emotions (i.e. regulate). This may consist of calmly talking children through emotions, giving them the responsibility to gain control by telling them when they are or are not out of control. In addition parents can remove a child from a situation, help him/her regulate and adapt the emotions before returning.

Besides the specific techniques of regulating emotions, children learn other management skills. These are developed in part because children mature mentally while they are participating in a family's emotional style. Generally, children learn the same variety of emotions as are expressed in their families. Families who are more expressive will tend to have more expressive children. Families who are inhibited or restrictive will tend to have less expressive children.

While children enter their adolescence they are faced with the need to specialize their emotions, make emotional commitments to values, to other people, and to achievement. During this period, children refine how they display their feelings by making their private feelings the same as their public display. Sometimes adolescents will be so self-conscious during this period they will, because of security needs, disguise their feelings and mask them with behavior that does not reveal the true emotional experience. This condition, though common, limits development toward emotional maturity. When children learn EMOTIONAL HONESTY which means to tell and display outwardly what they feel internally; they will increase their movement toward more mature emotional behavior.

EMOTIONS AND EMOTIONAL WELL BEING

One prominent theory describing how to promote high self-esteem suggests that it (self-esteem) is related to positive emotions. That is, when children feel more love and less fear, more kindness and less anger, more security and less anxiety, they will also develop an overall confidence or trust in themselves. When this condition exists, children demonstrate the characteristics of high self-esteem.

This should mean to us that it will benefit children if they are exposed to more positive emotions than those we consider negative. As parents or teachers you may consider the amount of warmth you express, or optimism, happiness, cheerfulness, kindness, and love. When children receive these from caring adults they are more likely to learn how to express them. This will start a cycle which will be repeated not only in the child's life but in the next generation as well.

LEARNING ACTIVITIES

Objective: To refine your understanding of emotional development, promote your emotional maturity.

1. Write the definitions of the following terms:
   a. emotional state _____
   b. emotional display_____
   _____
   c. emotional experience_____
   _____
   d. emotional honesty_____
   _____

2. Describe how you display the following emotions:
   a. anger_____
   _____
   b. fear_____
   _____
   c. love_____
   _____
   d. happiness_____
   _____

3. Describe the emotions you best control and least control. Describe why you believe you are able to control some and reasons why you cannot control the others as well.
   _____
   _____
   _____
   _____

4. Select two people and ask each of them four questions. Record their answers.
   a. ask them to tell about an historical event they remember.
   b. ask them to tell about an activity they like
   c. ask them to talk about someone they know
   d. ask them to talk about themselves

* Answer the following questions about this exercise.

   1. Which question yields the most emotional information?_____
   2. How did each person display his/her feelings while talking about each question?__
   _____
   _____
   _____

3. Under which condition was each person the most expressive? The most restricted?_____
_____
_____
_____

5. Write a 3-4 page paper about emotional development. In your paper write, and give supporting examples, about the following topics.

    a. Describe immature and mature emotional behavior
    b. Describe the skills necessary for a person to develop toward increased maturity.
    c. Describe how and why children learn to adapt emotions from one situation to another.
    d. Describe your emotional style and evaluate where you are less and/or more mature. Give examples.
    e. Describe how you CAN improve our level of maturity.

SOCIAL LANGUAGE

Most people are familiar with and accept that geographic and cultural differences affect people's language. In the United States, for example, accent and word pronunciation are used by some to determine where the speaker "grew up". Yet we do not often think about the vocabulary and language style of children as they enter their social world. Social language is an interesting part of child development and through it one can see the formation of social behavior as children grow older.

Children formulate a language to talk about people, people's actions, games they play, and certain emotional events. Children also create special codes that exclude those who are not "as well liked" at that moment. They might adopt the style (accent, vocabulary, idioms) of someone especially admired. Lastly they create phrases to fit special occasions.

"Ring around the Rosies," and "eeny meeny miny moe" are examples of games or sayings. "Geek", "nerd", and "wimp" are descriptions of people. "Bummer" and "yuk" describe emotional reactions, and pig latin is an example of a code children use to speak to each other.

This social language is an important part of childhood society. When children use the same words to describe social events, it is a common reference and indicates that the speaker belongs or wishes to belong. The most well-known example of this is the vocabulary of adolescent groups. In American society, the actual words change over time, but adolescent vocabulary is constant. Current examples include "Valley Girl" language such as "groty to the max" (i.e. as bad as possible), and "awesome dude" (i.e. great guy). Other current words are "babe" which describes a pretty girl, "hunk" which refers to a handsome well-built boy, and the prefix "mega" to describe anything extra- ordinary. Teenagers who use these word show that they are aware of what other teens know and they display the social cues that evidence memberships in groups. Information about social language has mostly come from writers describing the middle childhood years. There is, however, some evidence that children's first words include a social or interpersonal vocabulary.

(Nelson, 1973) described a study where mothers recorded the first fifty words of children two years old and younger. It was apparent that the words could be logically classified into two groups. One group described objects and the other consisted of words. One might conclude from her writing that social language is a part of every child's language development. Further, children, from early on, show differences in verbal skills.

THE IMPORTANCE OF SOCIAL LANGUAGE

One important feature of all language is the increased freedom it gives to think and represent the world without having to use the actual objects or actually act out our thoughts. The development of social language permits children to interact with words and ideas instead of just their actions. For example, disagreements can be resolved by talking, instead of fighting. Children use language to project a social image and achieve social positions. We could observe that children who are hindered in the development of speech and language will also have some difficulty socially.

Social language permits children to form friendship bonds, to be included with other children, and to regulate themselves and others. Those wishing to help children succeed can be expressive toward them as situations are explained, conversant with them about their social experiences, and can teach them a social vocabulary that enables children to be aware and sensitive.

LANGUAGE AND ADAPTATION

Language is social in another sense. It is used, for example, to indicate that a person has recognized the need to make adaptions from one situation to another. We might laugh and speak in louder tones prior to going to church, but when in church, our language changes to more reverent tones in order to demonstrate we know where we are. Another example of this adaption is demonstrated in the word selection and voice tones used when we are around a close friend as compared to talking with someone less known who may have great importance. This adaption can be found in every language and is called adapting from the familiar to the formal. Besides changing language to demonstrate adjusting to different situations, language is used to help in making the adaptions. When children are growing they discover that language can help them alter their emotions. Suppose, for instance, that a child is overly angry at something which happens in his family on the way to school. His anger is so great that he cannot get over it. One of the methods of helping him change this feeling into another is to use language as a means of making the transition. Language usage in this instance is used to make emotional adaptations.

You can probably imagine how it is important for people to talk through emotional situations. Many, however, are taught something different. Some believe that it is improper to disclose personal information and therefore pretend they are able to avoid revealing anything. Such individuals discover they have more difficulty resolving emotional problems and changing one emotion into the other. Generally, those who can disclose about themselves have more success and satisfaction in social relationships.

SEQUENCE OF DEVELOPMENT

Stage I Social Vocabulary 0-3	Children begin social language by first acquiring a basic acquiring a basic vocabulary of people and social-emotional events. During this stage words are used in simple relationship to the actual event. "I love you", is accompanied by a gesture, for example.
Stage II Social Rituals 3-8	Vocabulary is tied to reoccurring social rituals. These include games, mealtime, classroom events, friendship experiences, and shared social events with adults. Children ask questions about social events and they begin to use the words of their age group.
Stage III Social Problem Solving 8-13	With an increased vocabulary and awareness, children use words as the means of interacting with one another. They are capable of solving problems and organizing social events. Through these activities, social language is used to create such social positions of "leader," "friend," "nice," etc. Language is used and interpreted to reflect an individual's social position compared to other children. First attempts including humor in social situations can be observed.
Stage IV Social Identity Styles 13-	Social language is used as a symbol of group membership. Children's vocabulary is expanded to include numerous social situations. Styles of language can be adapted to specific situations (e.g. adult-child, authority figure, etc.). Individuals can be characterized by the style of language they express.

LEARNING ACTIVITIES

I. <u>Childhood language games</u>

<u>Objective</u>:   To collect samples of childhood games.

A. Interview several people to collect language games used by them in their childhood. Obtain verbal expressions for the following situations.

1. When children choose sides for a game.
   _____
   _____

2. When children decide who will be first.
   _____
   _____

3. When children ridicule other children.
   _____
   _____

4. Chants children use in playing social games (e.g. London Bridge is falling down).
   _____
   _____

5. Names children use for people they like.
   _____
   _____

6. Names children use for people they don't like.
   _____
   _____

7. Expressions of pleasure.
   _____
   _____

8. Expressions of dislike.
   _____
   _____

B. Create a friendly new nickname for people and use it with your friends. See if other people begin to use it (e.g. "spunkbubble" is a name for a nice person in Australia).

II. Personal Evaluation

Objective: To help you identify social situations where you exhibit expertise or where you need improvement.

A. Individuals are more calm if they have developed social language skills to help them express themselves adequately. We are more anxious when we are in a situation and cannot express ourselves adequately. Record the amount of tension you feel in the following situations.

1. Talking with a member of the opposite sex, whom you do not know well.

    Not tense   1   2   3   4   5   Very tense

2. Talking with someone who has authority over you.

    Not tense   1   2   3   4   5   Very tense

3. Talking over a disagreement with a friend.

    Not tense   1   2   3   4   5   Very tense

4. Talking to an audience of 50 people or more.

    Not tense   1   2   3   4   5   Very tense

5. Telling your feelings to someone close to you.

    Not tense   1   2   3   4   5   Very tense

B. Work out a plan to improve your social language. Select words or statements that will adequately describe:

1. Compliments you give to others.
2. Your own excitement or enthusiasm.
3. Descriptions rather than judgements of other people

C. Use these statements three times each in the next week. Record and report the results.

WHY CHILDREN DO WHAT THEY DO

You may not understand why your child acts a certain way, but there are reasons. It is important to understand these different reasons: you can be more successful with a given child if your approach towards him is consistent with the reason for his action.

One set of parents had a son who frequently wet his pants, even though he was six and a half years old. They tried to be patient, but eventually they gave in to shaming, spanking, or grounding him. Nothing seemed to work. Seeking help from a counselor, they were asked to subject the child to a physical examination. Results showed that the child had a very small bladder--so small, in fact, that he could not retain urine for any appreciable amount of time. Had the parents known the reason for the behavior, they could have been more successful and would not have been so destructive to their child.

BEHAVIOR DUE TO A STAGE OF DEVELOPMENT

Behavior may be attributed to a stage of development. Certain cues help identify behavior caused by a developmental stage. First, you can remember behaving similarly at that stage of your own life; if you can remember, you can be sure that your child's behavior isn't peculiar to him. It might really be behavior that is prompted by a stage of growth common to all children.

A second cue is if you have seen the same behavior in other children of the same age. A scoutmaster who was having problems of rowdiness with his twelve and thirteen-year-old scouts came home from a scout meeting and told his wife, "I just don't understand these boys. And the funny thing is that the boys I had last year were the same. And the scouts I had five years ago were doing the same things." This scoutmaster should probably attribute the rowdiness to a stage of growth. But if you're going to use this cue, you need to have seen a lot of behavior. You can be confused by thinking, "Okay, I saw such-and-such once, so I know that's what all children are like." Imagine, for example, a student teacher who goes to a room where the full-time teacher is a regular dictator. The students come in, sit at their desks, place their hands on the top of the desk, and sit looking straight ahead. They do not chew gum, talk to their neighbors, or leave their seat until the bell rings. The children, because they are frightened of their teacher, are models of good behavior. The student teacher might come back from his experience of a week and say, "Boy, eighth graders are at the greatest age in the world! I can't believe how well-mannered, polite, and quiet they are." If so, this student teacher has made two mistakes. First, he has not observed enough eighth graders to make a valid judgement about what all of them are like. Most eighth grade children are much more active; in fact, they are at one of the most difficult ages for growing children--they are pushing limits and trying to tell the world that they are not children any more. Second, the student teacher had never observed the behavior of those same eighth graders under less restricted conditions. Children who are coerced, who live in fear, or who have a poor environment probably will not act like children who live in normal conditions.

Recognizing the third cue requires that you have read about child behavior. Taking courses in child development and reading about what is expected in normal children helps you establish norms and helps you know what kinds of behavior you can expect from your child at certain ages.

The fourth cue is that the behavior may simply feel right to you. You may not remember it in your own life and might not have seen it happen or read about it, but instinct tells you that the behavior is appropriate for the child's age.

When behavior is caused by a stage of growth, it looks like the curves below.

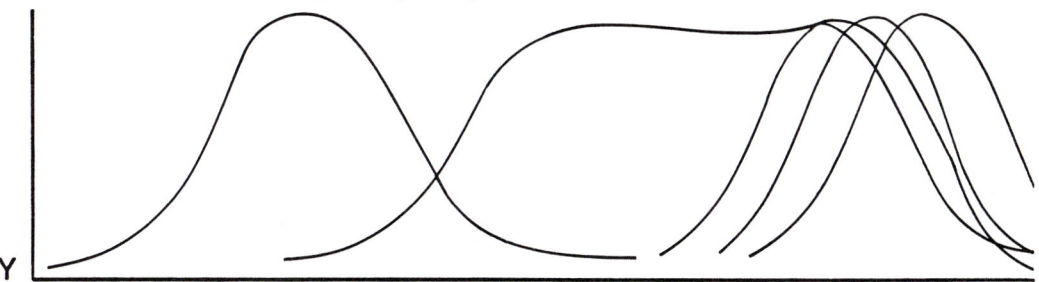

INTENSITY

TIME

The behavior starts out hardly ever occurring, reaches a peak, and then drops back to nothing. Sometimes a child is in a stage for a short time; sometimes for a long time. Sometimes several stages develop. Consequently, when you have decided that your child's behavior is caused by a stage of growth, you should not blame yourself for it. You didn't cause it; the cause lies within the child. The best thing you can do is to wait the behavior out until growth changes it. Be patient and know that the behavior won't last forever; realize that it will be there for a while and that it will then go away. And know, too, that other parents are experiencing the same thing, or something very similar, with their own children.

Although children sometimes pass through good stages, parents are often unaware of them, attending instead only to those stages that they think are negative. Many times parents aren't even aware that their child is going through a "good" stage.

In other words, the best cure for disturbing behavior that is caused by a stage of growth is to RELAX. If you can't relax, then try to channel the child into some other behavior that you can stand. If you do stop a particular behavior, you ought to make it clear that you are stopping it because of factors within you. If an action is a result of a developmental stage, the child is not bad; it is just that you cannot let your child act that way. If the action is a result of a stage of growth, try to be patient; the behavior will change by itself.

UNFILLED NEEDS

Unfilled needs are a second cause of behavior. When the child's needs are not fulfilled, an internal mechanism pushes him to seek fulfillment.

When a child's needs are unfilled, he will engage in attention seeking behavior. This is a plea by the child for someone to help him fill his need. If the need continues not to be met, the child's disturbing behavior will accelerate and look like the following.

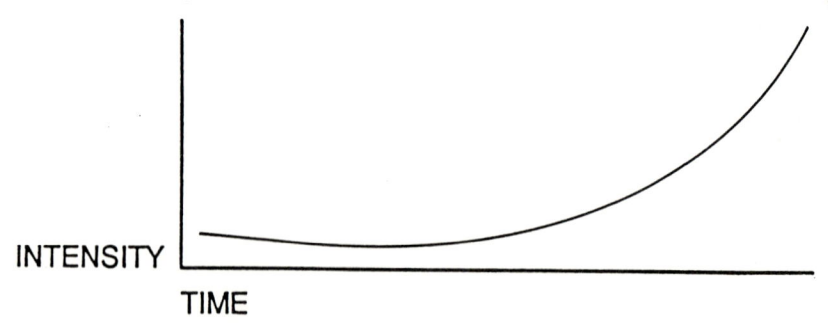

Notice that the disturbing behavior increases dramatically as time goes on. Behavior caused by an unfilled need will not go away on its own. It will only get worse. A list of the most important needs a child has is found in the reading "Innate Needs."

Just as there are cues for behavior caused by stages of growth, so there are cues for behavior caused by a desire to fulfill needs. The first cue, and possibly the most important, is that the behavior seems inappropriate for the age of the child. A nine-year-old child who is dragging a teddy bear around is an example of this. The child is waving a red flag, saying, "Help! I need some kind of nourishment."

Second, his behavior has an electric, supercharged quality to it. You may have known children who were so tense and anxious that whenever you touched them, you almost expected an electric shock. Unless they have physical problems, children who are overly active, who run or jump excessively, or who are unable to concentrate may be struggling to fulfill a need.

A third cue of unfilled needs is when the behavior doesn't occur in just one situation--when the behavior manifests itself at home, at school, at church, or at play. The child is trying to satisfy his needs everywhere.

A fourth cue is when bad behaviors keep popping up. Even though you may be able to train the child to discontinue one behavior, another behavior will take its place if the basic need is still there. In much the same way, when a person has an infection that manifests itself as a boil on his neck, he can put salve on the boil and clear it up, but another one may appear on his knee. And when he clears that one up, it breaks out again on his elbow, and so on, until the infection--the cause of the boil--is removed. Similarly, when there is an unfilled need inside, prompting bad behavior, the behavior will not go away until the need is filled. When the cues indicate an unfilled need, you must ask yourself, "What's my child trying to tell me? What isn't he getting out of life?" And when you have the answer, you must then satisfy his need.

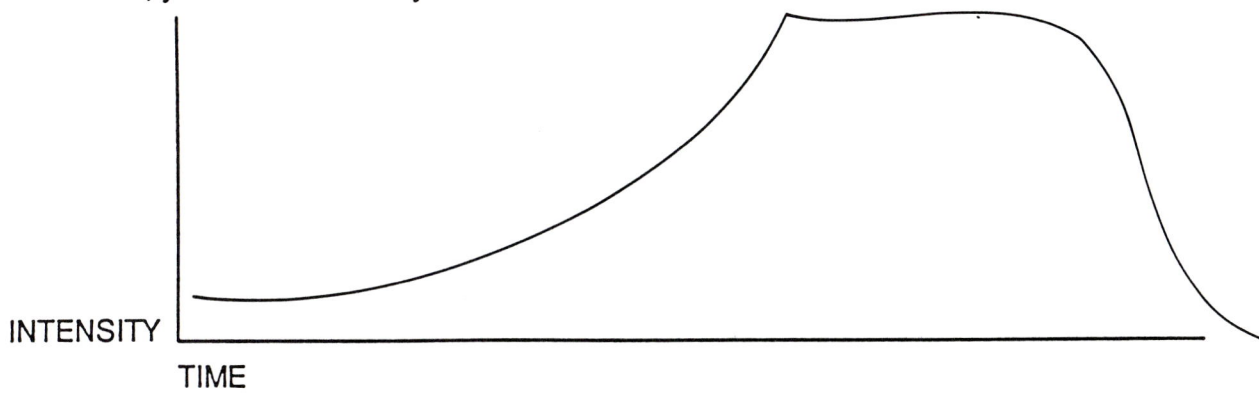

INTENSITY

TIME

The cure for behavior caused by an unfilled need is to fill the need. When a parent starts to do this, he may see no improvement in his child's behavior for quite a while. The child often tests his parents to see if they are sincere in their behavior. Once the child is convinced that his needs are going to be taken care of, his behavior drops off dramatically, as shown above.

A CHILD'S ENVIRONMENT

The third cause of behavior is some cue or event in the child's environment. If a child begins acting strangely and if none of the above cues explain the behavior, you may need to examine the present environment of your child. Who is present? How are they acting? Or ask yourself if anything traumatic has happened. Did the child move into a new school? Did a parent die? Was there a divorce in the home? Did he lose a best friend, or was there a fight with somebody at school? If you can pinpoint dramatic things that happened at about the time that the child's behavior suddenly changed, you've probably found the cause.

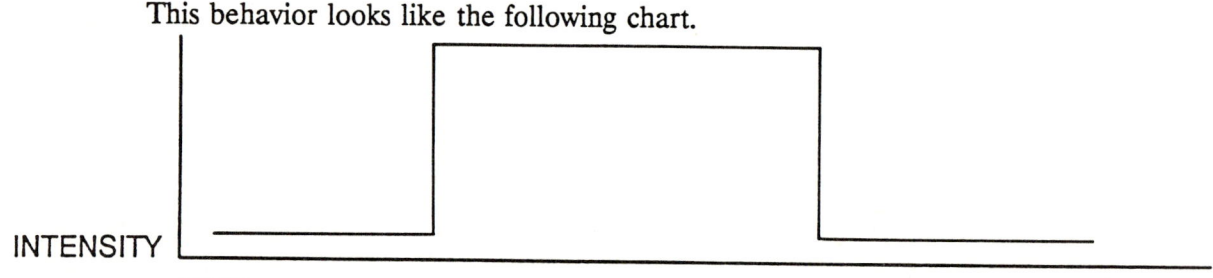

This behavior looks like the following chart.

In this case, a child didn't cause the situation; forces outside him probably did. And so, instead of growling, "That's a dumb way to behave," a better approach is to be a forerunner for your child--to sweep the stones and the stumbling blocks out of his way. If there is trouble with somebody at school, go and be his advocate. Learn about the situation and then communicate your support to the child. Maybe it means that you will even need to change. But one thing to be careful about is not to allow a child to be irresponsible. If the child brought about something in his environment, he must learn to pay the consequence.

The cure for disturbing behavior is to first try and undo the traumatic event. A child who has been transferred from one home room to another could be transferred back again.

But you can't undo a death or a divorce, and so the second cure is to try and cope with the situation by listening to the child, helping him understand what has happened to him, and helping him work out a plan to solve the problem. When this is successful, a child's bad behavior stops immediately. It looks like a miracle.

A LACK OF KNOWLEDGE: IGNORANCE

The fourth cause of behavior is simply that the child doesn't know any better. There are two causes for this. First, in families with many children, parents can lose track of which lessons they've taught each child; as a result they may have forgotten to teach a child a particular lesson. If none of the other listed causes seem to account for the child's behavior, you might decide, "Maybe I'm to blame for this because I didn't teach my child." If you are to blame, don't nag the child; sit down and teach him what he should do instead. By instilling good behavior, you help the child conquer the undesirable behavior.

There are many reasons why parents may fail to teach a child. Work demands, too many children, and tension in the family are some of the hindrances to teaching that are most commonly reported by parents. But, as we stated elsewhere, parents cannot not teach. Parents need to either take the effort to help a child learn correct behavior, or they risk having to deal with undesirable behavior. Even a few minutes of teaching each week can make a great difference in a child's behavior.

The second cause of a child not knowing what to do occurs when two parents tell him conflicting things. He becomes confused and not sure which he should do. Alternatively, a child can be confused when a parent acts hypocritically--telling the child to do one thing but doing the opposite himself.

The cure for this cause is obvious--teach the child and create a clear, consistent environment.

CONCLUSION

There are four causes of behavior: (1) developmental stages, (2) needs of the child, (3) something in his environment, and (4) the child's lack of knowledge. Of the four causes of behavior, only the first is determined by the child, and he isn't aware of the developmental stage he is going through. The other three causes are beyond a child's control; a child doesn't create a hunger inside, manipulate his environment, know everything. If he didn't bring the causes about, you shouldn't be angry with the child. Knowing the different causes of behavior and using the cues to identify them can help you to relax, to know how to best provide help, and to enjoy your child more.

TEACHING CHILDREN ABOUT SEX AND REPRODUCTION

Sustaining life in all its many aspects is a foundation principle of the gospel of Jesus Christ. It is our Father's work and glory to prepare us for an eternal <u>life</u>, full and abundant. He made the concept of life, its growth and progress; and death its opposite, physical and spiritual, recurring themes written in the scriptures. We are often exhorted, for example, to choose the way of <u>life</u> and avoid anything death producing. Furthermore, as we understand the concept of life we believe in successive stages of changing life forms and preparing for the progression from one form to another.

One's life, a fusion of intelligence and spirit, began as an offspring of divine and exalted parents. This unembodied spirit form combines with a body to fulfill mortal laws and opportunities. When the form of life again changes, it is to a separation of the body from the spirit that is still learning and progressing. Finally, life in its highest form begins after resurrection.

It is quite clear that we are eternal beings. That are, in mortality, vessels of life, and that we are to learn and make choices that permit us to continue living in joy and peace. Specifically, we must learn the laws of mortal life and satisfy the challenges here.

In our pre-mortal existence we did not have the power to act as a creator of anyone's life. But having been given the right to become like our eternal parents, we have, as part of mortality, had sown within us a biological drive and a soul-felt desire to procreate. This drive and desire are inherent within the body of every mortal being, and they are divine. This means that we are to have an active role in the formation of one part of life for someone other than ourselves. Indeed, our own eternal lives may literally depend on how well we manage our power to procreate while in mortality. Support for this idea can be shown in the following example.

Virtually every advanced species of animal life have a selection process to determine those fit and prepared to give life to other species members. With each season of mating, challenges exist where each is tested to determine the strongest who will be allowed to sire offspring. In this way the characteristics of the strong are added to the species and the failings of the weak are excluded. This example makes it quite easy for us to imagine eternal being who have gone on before us whose primary work is to create life and procreate it. These eternal parents are now determined to identify those of their children who will be given the same right to create and promote life forever and add to an eternal race of exalted beings. Only the strong and prepared will be given this right to add their genetic characteristic to the eternal race.

One can further reason this process of selection for us, in contrast to challenges animals face, includes how we manage the power to give life as mortal beings. Those will be chosen who keep this power within appropriate limits, using it righteously to promote the life of others. Those who turn the power of life into selfish abuse will not be selected. It is not a surprise that the greatest gift God can give is eternal procreation which is the reward for the valiant; instead of wealth or power or some other blessing. God's gift to Abraham (who was valiant) was the right to father innumerable decedents.

It is not difficult either for one to sense that the need to protect and preserve the power to give life is one of mortalities greatest challenges. The importance of this task requires that as parents, we give it our energy and emphasis in regard to our own lives and we are responsible to prepare our children so that they may use this power and desire in a righteous manner. Our adversary wishes to prevent us from succeeding by encouraging the use of this power for the purely selfish purpose of sensual pleasure. If we do so the precious work of our eternal parents will be frustrated. For it is true every abuse of the power to give life leads in the direction of death, the inability to procreate. Promiscuous behavior often results in disease that can permanently destroy procreation. Other sensual pleasure such as drug abuse destroys the desire and can alter the genetic composition of offspring making the continuation of life more difficult.

HOW PARENTS TEACH IS AS IMPORTANT AS WHAT IS LEARNED AND WHEN

Attitudes and values about something are most often learned by how we choose to teach more than what is taught. For example, if a parent teaches sexual information in an embarrassed or nervous way, there is a good chance children will assimilate these same feelings about sex. Or, if parents believe sex is evil and view it as base and animalistic, these attitudes may also be communicated. This implies that the first step in teaching children needs to be a preparation of ourselves. We can learn to explicitly say the parts of the male and female anatomy and can practice saying these and other terms until we feel comfortable doing so with our children. Someone suggested the idea to turn on the shower and say these words out loud until one felt no embarrassment. You may laugh when you read this, but it is a fairly good suggestion.

As you begin to formulate your method of teaching, try to begin by keeping in mind the ends you desire to accomplish. You might, for example, decide that the objective is to form a relationship with your children where both you as parents and your children could freely talk. Subsequently, whenever your children ask questions you can first reinforce them for coming to you and then try to tell them what they want to know.

In addition to wanting them to have an accurate factual knowledge about sex, another objective might be to have your children learn from both parents if both are available. There is much sons and daughters can and should learn from both parents. Both can be present in formal teaching times. Both will be asked questions by your children. A third goal is to teach some things at different times depending on a child's readiness to learn. Lastly, in addition to believing that sex is a source of joy in this life, we suggest that most parents want their children to have a deep understanding that their bodies and the power of creating life is a sacred trust and that expressing sexual love regularly and properly is necessary to form a lasting bond with their loved one. To understand this, they must learn to avoid seeing sexual impulses as something to only be controlled, which is an important trait in our view. They must learn, too, that they need to control themselves as a means of preparing to make a relationship with a married partner the best it can possibly be. One cannot have the fullest sexual experience, when appropriate, if there are not times when sexual desire is constrained. Not having something pleasurable at one time increases the intensity when experienced at another time. There is considerable evidence that he best sexual relationships are those where people live standards of sexual behavior consistent with our values as Latter-day Saints. That is, sexual behavior with someone only occurs in a context of deep emotional commitment for the purposes of procreation and bonding two people together.

A TEACHING PROGRAM

The following table contains some information about developmental stages of children and some suggestions for what to teach during each of our stages. Also show are some suggested ways to teach children.

	Development Stages of Children's Understanding	Concepts that Parents can Teach	Suggested Ways to Teach
FIRST CONCEPTS IN CHILDHOOD	About 0-7 years of age children are curious and think about objects and their physical properties such as shape, texture, size, and color. Children also organize ideas into concepts. (i.e. what parts does a boy have or a girl). They want to know about sensations associated with objects.	1. Teach about body parts using correct terms and differences between males and females. 2. Teach when to talk about parts of the body and when not to talk. (i.e. at home with parents and not primary class). 3. Teach concepts of modesty, and how wonderfully our bodies are made. 4. Begin principles of conception, pregnancy, and child prenatal growth.	1. Use baths or showers and children's questions as times to teach about the body. 2. Verbally explain times it is best to talk. 3. Use examples and positive comments about your own body and child's body to teach modesty and self-respect 4. Use reading material about pre-natal growth and childbirth. Use own pregnancy if appropriate. 5. Be loving, touch and give affection.

	Development Stages of Children's Understanding	Concepts That Parents Can Teach	Suggested Ways to Teach
EMOTIONAL CONTROL AND PRE-PUBERTY PHYSICAL DEVELOPMENT	From ages 7-11, children learn preliminary logical thinking, social skills, achieving a sense of relationships to other people, and learning to control emotions associated with personal life and social contacts.	1. Teach about conception (sperm and egg unite) and reproduction. 2. Reinforce the need to talk openly with parents about questions children might have. 3. Use social events to teach modesty and appropriate conversation. 4. Help children learn to control their emotional impulses, to avoid extreme or uncontrolled displays, be loving, learn to touch, and give affection.	1. Initiate conversation to learn about what a child knows. Reinforce your need to have a child talk to you. 2. Respond to questions as asked. 3. When a child exhibits extreme emotions, focus on the need to manage his/her impulses by sitting on a chair, until calm, cooling off in a bedroom, and talking about his/her feelings.

	Development Stages of Children's Understanding	Concepts that Parents can Teach	Suggested Ways to Teach
PUBERTY AND EARLY ADOLES- CENCE Ages 11-15	1. Increased interest in the body and in relating a person's body to such things as popularity, athletic skill, and attraction to opposite sex. 2. Increased awareness of physical changes and comparing themselves to others. They notice voice change, breast development, height, and hair on the body. 3. Increased self-consciousness about "looks" and ability to relate how they look to other things such as other's respect and social values. 4. More importance is given to opinions of peers. 5. Children experience strong sexual desire for the first time. 6. Children can mentally see the logic behind reasons, they perceive cause and effect relationships.	1. Teach about the changes that occur in puberty (i.e. menstruation, rapid growth that can be related to poor coordination, widening of shoulders and narrowing of hips for boys. A widening of hips for girls, enlargement of breasts for both boys and girls development of body hair under arms, and pubic area, and on boys' faces and arms). 2. Teach that "good looks" does not make a good person and one must develop good values, standards of personal conduct and modesty. 3. Teach social skills (how to make friends and talk with others) so that popularity is achieved on some basis other than physical attraction. 4. Teach that individuals go through puberty at different rates: some early, some later, some rapidly, some slowly. 5. Teach that our bodies and spirits are God's greatest earthly creation, and to respect ourselves is to respect Him.	1. Obtain good reading and other information to use with your family (elementary schools will have a good filmstrip). 2. Reinforce changes in children as positive by paying positive attention to their growth (e.g. "you sure have broad shoulders.") 3. Create teaching times where children are told about what to expect for boys and girls during puberty. 4. Share some of your own experiences with puberty and its changes. 5. Initiate numerous conversations to ensure development of positive attitudes about a child's body, social success, and personal standards. 6. Frequently ask what ideas your children have about themselves. 7. Teach ways to manage sexual desire. (i.e. avoid pornography, become involved in physical work, and conversation about fees used to increase popularity will achieve temporary results.

	Development Stages of Children's Understanding	Concepts that Parents Can Teach	Suggested Ways to Teach
Ages 15-18	1. Children can observe how they relate to others

2. Reasons and ideas must appear logical to be accepted

3. Perceived ability to make their choices is necessary for development of personal values. Attempts to force ideas will evoke resistance.

4. Social success increases in importance: especially attention from the opposite sex. Personal esteem is closely tied to feelings of being socially successful.

5. Children require abundant positive emotional support from parents.

6. Although children can understand correct principles, most have difficulty acting according to what they believe. | 1. Teach relationship of sex as a commitment to another person in marriage.

2. Too much sexual involvement too early cheapens and can ruin the companionship.

3. Physical attractiveness used to increase popularity will achieve temporary results.

4. How to hold expressions of intimacy within appropriate limits according to the state of responsible and legal commitment.

5. Sexual desire well managed is a major part of preparing for success in marriage.

6. Techniques for avoiding compromising situations (one father gave a dime to his daughter with this instruction: "If a boy wants to go too far, give him the dime and ask him to call me. Tell him if I say it's OK then you can go ahead.") | 1. Share personal experience showing correct choices.

2. Ask children to tell you their decision about keeping chastity and virtue. Ask, "what have you decided to do?"

3. Emphasize positive examples of young people marrying properly.

4. Initiate long talks about affection, sex, and relationships with others.

5. Express a confidence, support and love.

6. Tell children clearly what you want for them and why without demanding or threatening.

7. Avoid critical comments about their looks, choices, or actions. Instead focus on desirable things you want them to do. |

LEARNING ACTIVITY

Write a two page paper which describes in detail the following: 1) what you must know about sex yourself, 2) steps you will follow in teaching your children about sex.

CULTURE AND CHILD DEVELOPMENT

Usually, as children grow their understanding expands from the parent/child relationship, to the immediate family, to an extended family, to their friends on the street and neighborhood, to their town or city, to their state and country. As their participation in the activities of growing up increase, their understanding of their culture also increases. Family, media, church, schools, and friends transmit information about culture and how to participate in it. Child development is, therefore, influenced by culture. To understand child development, it is useful for us to be knowledgeable about how children develop in a cultural context.

THE CULTURAL CONTEXT

Every culture has common ingredients. Each has a language and a system of communication, kinship relationships, customs and traditions, some form of government, formal laws which govern everyone, and informal rules which, though unspoken, exert considerable influence over how people act. In addition, the laws or rules in any culture are reinforced by disapproval and approval mechanisms. When children comply they receive approval and when they do not, they receive disapproval. Examples of approval may be affection or attention. Disapproval may include shunning, family punishment, imprisonment.

In addition to the foregoing, a culture may have one or more religions which serve the purpose of giving direction to desirable behavior. Lastly, the people in any culture may share some characteristics in common (e.g. language) but differ from one another in other respects. This is the diversity aspect of culture. To understand culture, therefore, we must appreciate how diverse and how similar are the peoples in the culture.

PARTICIPATION IN THE CULTURE

In a context made up of these elements then, children are born and reared. Their early family experiences are principally designed to teach them how to later participate in each aspect of their culture. They learn language, for example, and participate in kinship relationships. With their relatives they learn how to participate in the customs or their culture. They discover approval and disapproval mechanisms and learn about conforming or non-conforming. They may also have experiences with fads and fashions which change from time to time.

The extent of a culture's influence on children depends upon how much or how well any given child participates in activities which are part of their cultural tradition. If a child cannot use language well, for example, he or she may not be able to benefit from the learning or training experiences of the culture in which the language is a part. Consider also, the idea that education is a means of transmitted cultural ideas. If any child does not participate meaningfully in educational activities, his/her participation in the culture may be limited.

CULTURAL NOTIONS ABOUT CHILD DEVELOPMENT

Like any value, a culture will have some values or attitudes about child rearing and child care. These are taught in educational settings, demonstrated in methods of child care, and presented in the media. For example, Japanese parents are more likely to keep their children physically close to them than children from the United States during the first three years of life. In the U.S. we value individuality and often treat our children in this manner. We also share some concept of what is "good" parenting or "bad" parenting. In any culture when people demonstrate incompetent parenting, they receive disapproval from other cultural members. In similar ways, we may be approved of for parenting in the way each culture deems to be appropriate.

Beyond the foregoing, culture and child development are related in other ways. For example, the members of each culture informally establish certain times when development milestones should be demonstrated. Anyone watching a child develop will measure the development by whether these milestones are manifest at about the times expected. In the United States, eighty percent agree that the best age for a man to marry is between 20-25. The best time for a woman is 19-24 years of age. A young man is someone between the age of 18-22 and most think schooling should end between the ages of 20-22.

Parents who are members of a culture will have awareness of these milestones and will often attempt to prepare their children to satisfy them. When children demonstrate the developmental milestones at the appropriate time parents often feel more successful than when children do not.

CULTURE, PERSONALITY, AND VALUES

All the participation in cultural events by parents and children inculcates values and ideals into each person about themselves and about the culture itself. As a result we get a "national" personality where members of a given culture share some common traits. Europeans may think, for example, that Americans are rich, somewhat unrefined or vulgar, loud and aggressive. Americans may think that Latin Americans are lazy, late, passionate, and/or unintelligent enough to remove themselves from poverty. Europeans and Americans may think Oriental people are shrewd, inscrutable, hard working, and pagan.

John Spielberg described some of these cultural value as they affect personality (social) development. He compared three nationalities: American, Oriental, and Latin American. He compared their values according to authority, orientation toward time, and orientation toward nature.

	United States	Latin America	Oriental
authority	individualistic	autocratic	group
time	present-future	present	past-present
nature	subdue it	controlled by it	harmony with it

If we look at the table above, we can see that cultural values can be transmitted to individuals and influence their social development. We can imagine there will be other influences a culture will have on individual socialization. Consider the power that comes from the following ideas (1) everyone believes or does the same thing, (2) something must happen by a certain time because it is "expected" (3) also, suppose we think the same things in our culture are harmful to our family values. Forces resulting from ideas such as these are felt deeply by parents and affect how they participate in the social development of their children.

LEARNING ACTIVITIES

Objective: To improve your understanding of culture and how culture exerts influence on children's socialization.

1. Identify and describe the elements of a culture which may affect the family and its efforts to socialize children. (e.g. laws, media, religion, etc.)

2. Identify at least five approval and disapproval mechanisms in our culture which govern how parents treat children.

3. Describe what you think would happen when parents view the culture as hostile to their values for their children? What would be appropriate and what would be inappropriate?

4. From your understanding about culture, give explanations as to why people believe, feel, and act as they do.

5. Identify the types of influence parents feel from their culture about child development.

RULES

Rules are formed when a person tries to understand how two or more things are related. Trying to understand the relationship introduces us to "ruleness." There are cognitive rules like the way a child solves a problem or groups objects together. There are social rules for many situations and human relationships. There are also rules for games and play. Further, rules exist for the decisions a child makes as part of moral reasoning. In all of these cases, a rule is a statement of general principles which serves to guide behavior or enable behavior to be understood.

Children's understanding of rules and their response to them appear to undergo a developmental sequence very similar to other aspects of child development. By understanding children's comprehension of rules and how they are affected by rules, we can increase our ability to help promote their development.

Rules, according to Gagne (1977), are a natural part of child development. They are a basic element of thought which every child learns. This learning appears to be related to the development of language and cognition. Further, children learn about rules from many sources and their response to rules can be influenced by friends, family, and the amount of exposure to social situations.

Because response to rules is a part of child development, there are no situations or style of thought where rules are absent. There can only be differing rule forms or different responses to rules. Even if someone wishes to have "no rules" a situation has been created with the special rules of not having any.

An example of the way the family environment can influence children's response to rules is shown in the study of the way deviance and schizophrenia are created. Children who exhibited behavioral rules deviant from their parents are often reared by parents who are very inconsistent enforcers of rules and may even contradict one another. In this case, a child forms the rule that parental and societal rules may not apply to him.

Schizophrenia is a mental disorder when rules of thought the individual believes to be appropriate are not realistic. Such a person has rules, but they are an altered from what most "normal" people use. Some writers have shown that parents can transmit these "rules" of thought to children by the following: (1) Communicating that a certain rule exists and the child should follow it. (2) After the child follows a rule, he is criticized by a parent for following a rule the parent didn't create. (3) The parents prevent the child from telling of their parental inconsistency. When these "double bind" conditions exist the child tries to explain the situation to himself by formulating an irrational rule of thought.

    Just as one family environment can adversely affect children, a positive family can help children learn about varieties of rule forms and promote a child's use of them. This is made more probable when parents understand the developmental sequence of children's response to rules.

DEVELOPMENTAL SEQUENCE

Stage I
Single Concept Learning
Age 0-2

Children do not know that rules exist. They learn single concepts and relate to each one by itself. There are very few ritual games, social conventions, or styles of thought that a child is aware of. Consequently, a child is governed by demands Learning of people or situations.

Stage II
Rigid Adherence to rules
Ages 4-7

After developing the concept of rules they recognize that rules apply to several situations. Children exhibit the rudiments of rule-governed problem solving and social to exchange. Play becomes more formalized. Children consider rules, once established, to be sacred and untouchable. Changes in rules are made only if they appear to be "new" rules.

Stage III
Rule by Authority
Ages 7-11

Children apply concepts of rules to the authority of adults over them. Respected adults are responded to as if whatever they say must be so. Rules are, therefore, more than the way games are played or the way people act in public. Rules are connected to by authority and are used by those in authority to regulate others. Children's responses to rules are quite rigid. They accept few if any changes in explicit rules.

Stage IV
Flexibility and Cooperation
Ages 11 and older

Adult authority is no longer accepted without question. Children begin to adjust rules to fit the circumstances they are in. They may rearrange the rules of a game to better accommodate some player. Satisfying human concerns can be more and important than rigidly following the rules of a game. Children are able to create rules to suit their own unique purposes and include getting others involved to cooperate in making the rules. Diversity among children is more apparent and children can characterize one another by their willingness or unwillingness to cooperate in changing rules or creating new ones.

LEARNING ACTIVITIES

I. "Crazy Rules"

Purpose: To demonstrate the effects of inconsistent and inappropriate rule change.

A. Select a person you are comfortable with (friend) and ask for permission to try an experiment, say, "I am doing an experiment on planned inconsistency, I need someone to do it on for 5 days." Do the following:

1. Hypocrisy: Make at least three mutual agreements and then violate them giving a "good excuse" for doing so. Also say that you always keep a promise.

2. Contradictory Rules: Select something you see your friend do frequently and mildly praise it. Then at another time mildly criticize it by saying, "I'm not sure you should do that."

3. Excessive Rigidity: Work out a schedule of events with your friend that leaves little to chance. Attempt to organize every 10-15 minutes for at least one evening.

4. Unpredictability: Announce daily that you plan to do something at a specific time in the presence of your friend, then fail to do it.

B. Discuss the following questions with your friend:

1. What did you think my experiment was about?
   _____

2. How did you react when I didn't keep any of our agreements?
   _____

3. What are the effects on two people when crazy rules are applied?
   _____

4. How do you think children will be influenced if parents use crazy rules?
   _____
   _____
   _____
   _____

II. <u>Adjusting rules to fit the children</u>

<u>Objective</u>: To create a set of rule conditions that are appropriate for children of differing ages.

A. Assuming that you are or will become a parent, describe how you would adjust to satisfy children's responses to rules at different developmental stages.

Stage 1 - Describe a constructive plan of child discipline for children age 0-3 who may not understand rules.

Stage 2 - How would you "teach" rules to children?

Stage 3 - Describe what parents can do when children tie rules to adult authority. Why is parental consistency important?

Stage 4 - Describe how adolescents and their parents can achieve mutual consent about family rules. What are the consequences if parents are too rigid and allow no flexibility? What if parents are too flexible?

B. Show all of your ideas by writing them in a paper and turning it in.

A DYSFUNCTIONAL FAMILY

It is well known that family experiences affect the development of children. It has only been in the last few years, however, that researchers have systematically studied the family to determine how family influences the development of children. In that process we have learned some interesting things. One highly significant idea is that the actual effects of a family on children is determined by factors in the child as well as in the family. For example, some children with excellent family environment do not do well growing up and have struggles in many different ways. Further, some children in difficult family circumstances live and perform adequately. This tells us that to understand the role and influence of a family on children we must look at both family and children.

FAMILY DIMENSIONS

Most of us think about families as places where parents and children live together. So we think about the differences between families with one parent, or two parents, with one child or many children, all boys or girls. These descriptions usually do not help us identify dysfunctional families. There are other ways to distinguish those families which are dysfunctional from those which are effective. We can do this by evaluating family communication, work strategies, affection, rules, environmental sensitivity, leadership and relationship style.

Communication

All families are networks of communication. Families vary in how much information they communicate, whether they encourage everyone to participate, and what they communicate about. Families may also perpetuate communication problems where they interrupt each other, blame and criticize, speak sarcastically, or neglect communicating at all. Others may value communication highly so they avoid doing anything that will prevent positive communication from taking place.

Work

Families are places where work is required. Families may vary in how they divide the work (e.g. give everyone assignments), the standard of performance which is required, and how important work is compared with other family activities. For instance, some families work hard but also play hard. Others work more than they play and still others spend more time in leisure activity than they do with work.

Affectional System

The people in families develop and display regard and respect for one another. Some families may be openly demonstrative by touching, hugging, gazing at each other, and other forms of affection. Others may be less demonstrative and less open. The affectional system in families includes how families attend to emotional behavior of family members. In some families, feelings are expressed and understood while in other families emotions tend to be ignored or unexpressed.

Rule System

Families have formal rules which are organized and spoken about. They also have informal rules in the form of expected or routine practices. Some families will have many while others have only a few. In addition, families differ in terms of what they have rules about. One might have curfew rules and no rules about mealtimes while another would have rules about TV watching and none about getting their work done. Most families have a discipline system where parents or caretakers express approval or disapproval for what children do and how they act. Families can be understood in terms of how they establish a rule system and enforce it.

Environmental Sensitivity

Some families will explore their world and bring home interesting things to discuss and share. Others are less aware of their environment and might be frightened about it. Therefore they are less likely to venture out and learn. In addition, families can be understood in terms of the types of activities they participate in. Some may actively participate in religious activities while others participate in non-religious social activities.

Leadership and Relationship Style

Since there are people in families they form relationship styles. These relationships are demonstrated in the way leadership is exerted in the family. These may be democratic where most family members have a say in the way the family is governed. Another may be authoritarian where one parent or both make demands on children. In any event all families will have a leadership and relationship style which characterizes the family.

HOW DYSFUNCTIONAL FAMILIES DIFFER FROM EFFECTIVE FAMILIES

Having learned about some family dimensions we can proceed to our understanding of the characteristics of a dysfunctional family. The term "dysfunctional" means the family is not able to promote the positive development of its members. Instead family members are involved in ways which hurt their own and others growth. Researchers have given names to certain conditions which prevent positive development from taking place. Notice that these conditions exist because the family members do not have a broad or clear understanding of children and the knowledge of how to promote development.

Enmeshment

This dysfunctional condition exists when children believe their thoughts must be the same as other family members. Enmeshment is created in several ways. Excessive fear of disapproval is a leading cause. In addition, when families fail to recognize individual traits, needs, desires, emotions, of family members, then it is possible for one person to think he/she is simply like everyone else. In healthy families there is strong emphasis on both togetherness and individuality. Individuals are asked to make choices where they are primarily responsible. In addition, communication in the family allows for individual opinions.

Abuse

Abuse can be anything which removes a sense of self-control and self-confidence from anyone. In dysfunctional families there may be one or more types of abuse. These may be physical where an older bigger person physically hurts a younger, weaker person. Abuse may be emotional where words are demeaning and hurtful or affection and attention is withdrawn or used to exploit someone. Abuse may also be sexual where one person is used and exploited for the gratification of another without having a chance to make choices or be aware of the consequences of those events. In many instances, extreme levels of stress from outside pressures are related to the incidence of abuse. In healthy families, relationships are established for the welfare of individuals. Therefore, how they act toward each other is more moderate and non-exploitive. Methods of discipline are democratic and there is generally open displays of affection which continue and are not withdrawn as a result of misbehavior.

Excessive Dependency

Children begin life dependent on adults. This dependency is recognized and accepted because children are not able to care for themselves. As they mature, however, children typically want to do things for themselves and so make demands to do so. The parent-child attachment is sufficiently intense that unless parents and children are sensitive to the development of independence, children can learn excessive dependency. This is manifest by helplessness, inability to leave the home, passivity when in proximity to parents, failure to achieve, irresponsibility, deviance from family rules (which appears to require parents to exert control), confusion and indecision, and separation distress when leaving parents.

These conditions can be caused when parents do not encourage gradual separation between themselves and their children. Further, some parents assume excessive responsibility for their children and attempt to prevent failures by rescuing them from hurtful situations rather than let children solve their own problems. Parents also may indulge their children without setting behavioral limits and enforcing them. When children are indulged and have no standards to live up to, they acquire the belief that they need only be nice and pleasant to be adequate.

Dependency can be enduring. There is some evidence that dependent children become dependent adults. This means they will seek relationships with others which approximate the emotional conditions of their early family experience.

They may, for example, seek a marital partner whom they can be dependent upon and be uncomfortable when they are asked to act decisively and independently.

Mental and Emotional Illness

For many years, researchers did not make any connection between dysfunctional families and emotional and mental problems. Now, however, there is a clear link between such family problems as chemical abuse (forty percent of chemically abusing teens have parents who abuse chemicals such as alcohol and drugs). In addition, some forms of depression appear to be inherited; but other depression is learned from parent's examples. When families have communication which is not logical or based on reality, children can learn a form of irrationality which manifests itself in schizophrenic thought disorders. The family appears to believe something and children assume that it is factual because the whole family seems to believe it. A case like this is the famous Emmanuel David family where the father kept his children isolated from any source of information, proclaimed himself a prophet or the Holy Ghost and then on one occasion jumped from a hotel window followed by four of his children and his wife. They all jumped. Two children survived.

In contrast, healthy families have a fairly open communication system with the world around them. They may screen out information which does not promote their specific values but are usually aware of and communicate with people and institutions outside the family.

Incompetence

Some parents do not have basic child care or organizational skills. Therefore they ar not able to organize a family nor care for children in ways which promote development. In these cases, families do not have routines of care such as bedtimes or mealtimes. Nor do parents have methods which allow them to identify and respond to children's needs in terms of clothing, feeding, emotional support, etc. Children's physical and mental growth may be retarded. In addition, however, they may also have very limited ability to function in social situations and achieve educationally or at work.

Healthy families, of course, have effective child care methods and organize their families in ways which are conducive to healthy development. They have positive care routines, set predictable activities for the family, and nurture child growth.

LEARNING ACTIVITIES

Objective: To help you understand the dimensions of family organization, the characteristics of a dysfunctional family, and promote healthy family life.

1. Analyze your family of origin in terms of how your family managed the following:
   a. communication _____
   b. work _____
   c. affectional system _____
   d. rule system _____
   e. relationship style _____

2. Describe your ideal family using the dimensions described in this article.
   _____
   _____
   _____
   _____

3. Select (1) abuse, (2) dependency, or (3) enmeshment and answer the following questions about (e.g. abuse) the one you selected.
   1. What is the leadership or relationship style? _____
   2. What is the communication system like? _____
   3. What rules or lack of rules might exist? _____
   4. In what ways does the family show sensitivity or insensitivity to the environment? _____

4. Put all of the above in a paper and include a section which describes the difference between a healthy and a dysfunctional family.

THE ENDOCRINE GLANDS

All the physiological functions of humans are coordinated and regulated by the nervous system. To this system there must be added a special integrating mechanism of chemical regulation. These chemical regulators are called **hormones**, and are produced by **endocrine glands**. The endocrine glands play an especially important part in the organism in coordinating and regulating the physiological processes of the whole person.

The endocrine glands do not constitute an organ system, but are referred to as the endocrine system. These glands secrete their products directly into the blood stream for transmission to the various tissues. Hormones exert profound effects on certain tissues and are needed in relatively small amounts to produce their effect. The tissue on which a specific hormone exerts its effect is called the **target tissue**. A state of balance normally exists between the various glands, and a reciprocal interaction usually exists among them. One gland may at the same time stimulate simultaneously many glands which may produce a series of stimulations and inhibitions. Thus where one endocrine gland can stimulate another, the gland that is stimulated may have an inhibiting effect on the stimulator. As in the relationship between estrogen and FSH, when one decreases the other increases, and vice versa. It is important to have a basic understanding of how hormones work, because they play an important role in a person's physical growth and development, metabolism, reproductive cycle, sexuality, emotional life, and personality. We will briefly study the following endocrine glands: (1) the pituitary, (2) thyroid, (3) parathyroids, (4) adrenals, (5) pancreas, and (6) gonads.

The pituitary is located in the brain. Generally the gland is divided into the **anterior**, **intermediate**, and **posterior lobes**. The anterior pituitary secretes hormones that mainly influence other endocrine glands and best illustrates the reciprocal relationship that exists within this system. These hormones are referred to as **tropins** and are carried by the blood to other target glands, where they aid in the maintenance of the glands as well as stimulating them to produce their own hormones. Six hormones are secreted by this part of the pituitary: the growth hormone, the lactogenic hormone, the follicle-stimulating hormone, the luteinizing hormone, the thyrotropic hormone, and the adrenocorticotropic hormone.

The **growth hormone**, also known as **somatotropin** or **STH** functions to stimulate the growth of the long bones and muscles. Excess production of growth hormone during childhood or adolescence results in **gigantism**. Normally growth hormone is active only up to the time of maturity. Growth hormone in excess suppresses gonadotropic hormones. If the testes and adrenals in the male, or adrenal glands in the female, do not develop as in normal puberty, epiphyseal closure of the long bones, which is dependent on the male hormone, fails to take place, and a person can continue to grow to 7 or 8 feet.

Should the hyperfunction occur after epiphyseal closure, there is no further increase in linear growth but an increase in the width of bone. This results in an unusual thickening of the hands and feet, prominence of the jaw, and enlargement of the nose, and is called **acromegaly**.

Lactogenic hormone stimulates growth of the mammary glands; the **follicle-stimulating hormone** (FSH), stimulates the graafian follicle in the ovaries to mature and produce estrogen and stimulates sperm formation in the male; and the **luteinizing hormone** (LH) causes ovulation and development of the corpus luteum and production of progesterone in the female and stimulates testosterone production by the testis in the male. These hormones are essential at the time of puberty and throughout the reproductive life of the ovaries for continued graafian follicle development and ovulation. FSH is carried to the ovaries by way of the blood stream, where it stimulates the ovarian follicle to mature, and estrogen secretion is stimulated. As a result of estrogen secretion, changes occur in the secondary sexual characteristics. At the time of ovulation, which is initiated by the combined action of FSH and LH, the level of estrogen reaches its peak and suppresses the secretion of FSH. As the concentration of FSH in the bloodstream falls, its stimulating effect on the graafian follicle is decreased, and the secretion of estrogen is decreased. As the concentration of estrogen falls, more FSH is secreted, resulting in the development of another follicle and more estrogen secretion.

The lactogenic hormone seems to be responsible for causing the corpus luteum to produce progesterone. Since progesterone is necessary for the growth and maintenance of the endometrium in the uterus, it is necessary for the corpus luteum to be sustained until the embryo has been able to establish itself in the uterus and has begun to develop. If the corpus luteum is not maintained for any reason, the endometrium sloughs off as the menstrual flow, and if the woman is pregnant, the implanted fertilized ovum is carried away with the debris.

A reciprocal relationship exists between the levels of LH and LTH and progesterone similar to that which exists between FSH and estrogen. As the level of progesterone increases in the blood, the secretion of LH and LTH is suppressed. As a result, the corpus luteum begins to fade, and the concentration of progesterone decreases. If the egg is not fertilized, the supplemental supply of progesterone produced at the site of implantation in the uterus will not be forthcoming from the placental membranes, and the corpus luteum disintegrates and the endometrium sloughs off. The waning in the concentration of the progesterone stimulates the pituitary to secrete more LH and LTH.

The **thyrotropic hormone** functions to maintain the thyroid gland and stimulates it to produce the hormone thyroxine. Too much of this hormone causes excessive production of the thyroid hormone and thus produces all the symptoms of excessive thyroid activity (hyperthyroidism). On the other hand, a deficiency of thyrotrophic hormone causes the thyroid to atrophy.

The **adrenocorticotropic hormone** stimulates the secretion of cortical hormones by the adrenal cortex. Excess production of ACTH stimulates the adrenal cortex to produce steroids, which causes water retention in the face and gives a characteristic roundness of the face, sometimes described as "pig-eye" or "moonface." There is also usually an increased growth of hair on the face.

The **intermediate lobe** secretes a hormone known as the **melanocyte-stimulating hormone** or **MSH**. It acts in the dispersion of pigment granules in the melanocytes, which are important in the darkening of the skin, as in tanning.

The **posterior lobe** secretes two active substances: **vasopressin** and **oxytocin**. Vasopressin acts to elevate blood pressure by constricting the peripheral blood vessels, and also promotes resorption of water by the kidneys. It has been used in cases of surgical shock in conjunction with other drugs to elevate the blood pressure. Oxytocin stimulates smooth muscle contraction, particularly of the uterus. It is therefore used in obstetrics to prevent postpartum hemorrhage resulting from an overly relaxed uterus.

THE THYROID GLAND

In contrast to the pituitary gland, the thyroid gland has only two hormones: **thyroxine** and **triiodothyronine**. The primary action of thyroid hormones is on regulating the metabolic rate. These hormones directly increase the rate of oxidation of foodstuffs within the cells of the tissues. Many normal functions of the organism are dependent on thyroid secretion. These include water and mineral metabolism and the normal function of the nervous system, muscular systems, and circulatory system. All these functions are disturbed with either a deficiency or excess of the hormone.

Abnormalities associated with the thyroid gland are due either to a deficiency of iodine, the essential element of the thyroid hormone, or to an insufficient production of the hormone itself, or to an over-activity of the gland with the liberation of an excessive amount.

A deficiency of iodine in the diet is frequently accompanied by an enlargement of the gland, which is called a **goiter**. In this condition the thyroid is enlarged, apparently to compensate for the lack of iodine.

A deficiency of thyroid hormone, referred to as hypothyroidism, produces a number of symptoms depending on the degree of deficiency and the age at which it occurs. Lack of thyroid hormone in very early childhood leads to **cretinism**, a condition characterized by cessation of mental and physical development, slow heart rate, poor appetite, and constipation.

Thyroid insufficiency occurring later in childhood results in **juvenile myxedema**. The most characteristic symptoms are as follows: the child shows a tendency to be stout, short, and squatty; the head is proportionately larger than the normal for the age of the child and is attached to the trunk by a short neck. In the adult, hypothyroidism gives rise to the condition known as **myxedema**. In true myxedema the face is quite expressionless, puffy, and pallid. Both the mental and physical processes slow down.

Excessive thyroid function, known as **hyperthyroidism**, results from enlargement of the gland, with over-production and excessive release of thyroid hormone. The most characteristic symptoms in addition to goiter are nervousness, irritability, purposeless movements, fatigue, loss of weight, increased heart rate, elevated metabolic rate, and emotional instability.

THE PARATHYROIDS

The parathyroids produce a hormone that plays a vital role in the metabolism of calcium and phosphorus. The symptoms associated with hypothyroidism are muscle weakness, tetany, and irritability.

THE ADRENALS

The adrenals are two pyramid-shaped structures lying one on each side of the body, close to the upper part of the kidney. Each gland consists of two functionally distinct parts: a central portion, called the **medulla,** and a surrounding zone of tissue, called the **cortex.** The only function of the adrenal medulla is the secretion of **epinephrine.** In general, epinephrine has the same effect on a person as stimulation of the sympathetic nerves. The secretion of the adrenal medulla is under control of the sympathetic nervous system, and in emergency situations or exposure to stress, such as injury, excessive muscular exercise, infection, hemorrhage, cold, fever, burn, nervous shock, and anoxia, epinephrine is discharged into the blood. The increase of epinephrine, helps the organism to re-establish the physiological balance that has been disturbed. Prolonged stimulation can cause exhaustion of the epinephrine stores.

The **adrenal cortex** produces hormones which are necessary for life. The adrenal cortex produces many hormones but only three are of interest to us: cortisone, androgen, and estrogen. Cortisone helps maintain water balance in the tissues, and helps the body resist infection and cope with the effects of long-term stress. It is often a treatment for rheumatoid arthritis, rheumatic fever, and leukemia. The side effect of this hormone used therapeutically is that the body retains lots of water and the patient looks quite puffy. The adrenal cortex secretes both male and female hormones, and certain tumors of the adrenals cause the production of increased amounts of these hormones, giving rise to physical abnormalities, referred to as the **adrenogenital syndrome.** In the young male with adrenogenital syndrome, there is precocious development of the penis and pubic hair, along with advanced bone age and early and increased growth rate. A girl born with the adrenogenital syndrome may show an enlarged clitoris and may be mistaken for a male; thus she may be raised as a boy. In the adult female with adrenogenital syndrome there is repression of female characteristics with a prominence of male characteristics.

THE PANCREAS

The pancreas produces the hormone **insulin**. Insulin promotes the removal of glucose from the blood and makes it available to be converted to glycogen in the muscles and liver. An excessive amount of insulin in the blood, commonly results from improper insulin medication and occasionally from tumors. The resulting symptoms are caused by the fall in blood sugar, a condition referred to as hypoglycemia. A feeling of drowsiness and yawning usually occurs, and the hypoglycemic person may become excited or perspire or appear to be under the influence of alcohol. Convulsive seizures may occur, and finally the patient may go into coma and die. If adequate amounts of glucose are given to the person, the symptoms go away. The administration of insulin to diabetic patients rapidly restores the ability to oxidize carbohydrates and to form glycogen. When there is a deficiency of insulin, the utilization of glucose decreases but the level of blood glucose rapidly rises, producing a condition known as **hyperglycemia**, which results in a series of symptoms referred to as **diabetes mellitus**. Diabetes is a metabolic disease characterized by a disturbance in carbohydrate metabolism, protein, and fat metabolism. The disease usually leads to weight loss, kidney failure, and blindness.

GONADS

<u>Ovaries</u>. The two **ovaries** are situated deep in the pelvic cavity, one on each side of the uterus. Each ovary represents the female gonad in which the ova are produced. Within the ovaries are a number of ovarian follicles. It has been estimated that there are approximately 400,000 immature follicles in both ovaries at birth. Beginning at puberty, the follicles mature, one approximately every 28 to 30 days.

Deviations from the normal course of menstruation are not uncommon. **Menorrhagia** is a condition characterized by an abnormal loss of blood during the monthly period. It is usually caused by endocrine or ovarian functional disturbances. **Metrorrhagias** are irregular hemorrhages. The hemorrhage may appear before the menstrual period, in the middle of the interval, or after the menstrual period. **Amenorrhea** is the term used to denote the absence of menstruation. The most common cause of amenorrhea is pregnancy, but other causes can be excessive physical exercise or anorexia. The term **menopause** is that period in the female reproductive cycle when menstrual flow ceases. It can occur at any time after the menarche, but on the average the onset is at around 47 to 48 years.

If the ovaries of the normal female are removed before puberty because of some disease or have been rendered inactive by x-ray therapy, the child never develops the secondary sexual characteristics, and the sexual organs remain immature. Growth continues at a normal rate but does not show the usual spurt associated with puberty, and the individual ends up with the skeletal configuration typical of eunuchs; the length of the lower limbs is much greater than that of the trunk. Removal of the ovaries after puberty will also cause changes; the breasts usually atrophy, growth of hair on the face and body may occur, the body configuration of the female becomes more masculine, and sexual drive may decrease. The administration of estrogens is highly satisfactory in the treatment of eunuchoidism, as it will cause development of the secondary sexual characteristics.

<u>The Testes</u>. The testicles are two small, flattened, oval-shaped glands, which are situated in the **scrotum**. The testicles are composed of a number of **lobules**. Each lobule is composed of several **seminiferous tubules**. There are 800 or more tubules in the testicles. The testes, like the ovaries, have a dual function of producing sperm and sex hormone.

Hypogonadism is the condition of total loss of hormone activity of the testes. It occurs in castrated men and insufficient activity of the testes due to a deficiency of the pituitary. Castration before puberty or hypogonadism is usually followed by an excessive longitudinal growth of bones. Sex hormones stimulate the fusion of the epiphysis; thus in their absence there is a delayed fusion producing disproportionate growth of long bones. Hypogonadism in the male usually causes an accumulation of fat in the mammary region, around the hips, and below the waist. Early hypogonadism leads to a retardation of development of the penis, prostate, seminal vesicles, and vas deferens.

Hypergonadism refers to overactivity of the gonads, which leads to excessive development of the genitalia, secondary sexual characteristics, and the body as a whole.

Such men would have unusually broad shoulders, narrow hips, extremely muscular bodies, inordinately large sexual organs, and excessive body hair.

Many times children do not act exactly the way their parents think they should. They appear slow in their movements or they look lazy, or they seem to not be paying attention to what is going on, and many times this is caused by hormones inside of the child. When a parent assigns blame to the child as though they could control these behaviors, it makes the child's life miserable and he cannot do anything about that.

There is sort of a wisdom of the body that children discover very early. They adapt their life-styles and activities to what their bodies will allow them to do. Take for instance the case of a child who has low levels of thyroxin. They will be slow and lethargic, and any excess amount of activity, as in running races or something of that nature, totally depletes their energy source. As this child grows up and starts to play with children on the block or his cousins at reunions, and he engages in strong physical activities, his body pays a terrific price for that, so he learns to avoid those kind of things and picks out activities such as reading or working at a desk, where he doesn't have as much pain. The thing that parents need to do when a child has some kind of problem caused by a hormonal imbalance is first of all see if there is some remedial measure that can be corrected. If there isn't, they should be very patient and supportive of the child.

One of the developmental phenomena that are regulated by hormones is the age that somebody sexually matures, or goes through puberty. It would be nice if everyone's body matured at the same age, for instance on their thirteenth birthday. But that isn't how it works. People that deviate from the norm of physical maturation carry a lot of stress. For instance, an early developing girl--the first girl in a class that matures in fourth or fifth grade--or a late developing boy need a lot of support.

While growing up, one boy was very late in developing. It wasn't any fault of his. He happened to get some genes from his parents that dictated that to his body. When he was 17, his father, who also was a late developing boy, tried to give him some encouragement by saying, "Don't worry that you're smaller than your friends. I grew six inches when I was 22." Unfortunately this boy heard the last part of the sentence and not the first part, and nearly jumped off the roof of his house. He told his dad, "If I have to wait till I'm 22 to finally grow up and look like other guys, I'm just going to kill myself."

The principle to remember is that parents need to be informative and supportive. It is not very helpful to over-react by racing around trying to find doctors who will correct abnormalities in the hormone system that are within the normal range of deviation.

GLAND	HORMONES	FUNCTIONS	DEFICIENCY	EXCESS
Anterior Pituitary	Growth Hormone or Somatotropin	Controls growth of bone & muscle; anabolic effect on nitrogen metabolism; carbohydrate and fat metabolism; elevates glycogen stores of skeletal & cardiac muscles	Dwarfism	Giantism acromegaly
	Thyrotropic Hormone	Controls the rate of iodine uptake by thyroid tissue and influences the synthesis of thyroxine from diiodotyrosine	Atrophy of thyroid	Enlargement of thyroid
	Adrenocorticotropic Hormone	Stimulates the secretion of cortical hormones by the adrenal cortex	Atrophy of adrenal cortex	Unknown
	Prolactin or Lactogenic Hormone	Controls proliferation of the mammary gland and initiation of milk secretion; prolongs the functional life of the corpus luteum, the secretion of progesterone	Infertility	
	Gonadotropin	<u>Ovary</u> Controls formation of corpora lutea, secretion of progesterone; probably acts in conjunction with FSH <u>Testes</u> Stimulates the interstitial cells of Leydig, promoting the production of androgen	Infertility	
	Follicle-Stimulating Hormone (FSH)	<u>Ovary</u> Controls growth of ovarian follicles; functions with LH to cause estrogen secretion and ovulation <u>Testes</u> Has possible action on seminiferous tubules to promote spermatogenesis	Infertility	

GLAND	HORMONES	FUNCTIONS	DEFICIENCY	EXCESS
Posterior Pituitary	Antidiuretic	Affects water content of tissues; increases blood pressure	Excessive urine formation	Unknown
	Oxytocin	Stimulates uterine contraction; stimulates milk-producing cells of the mammary glands	Slow labor	Unknown
Thyroid	Thyroxin	Regulates general metabolism	Cretinism in children; lowered metabolic rate; weakness	Exophtalimic goiter; increased metabolic rate; weakness
Pancreas	Insulin	Carbohydrate metabolism	Diabetes mellitus; insulin shock; diabetic coma	Hunger & weakness; uses up sugar
Adrenal Cortex	Cortisone	Maintains: a) water balance in tissues b) carbohydrate balance c) resistance to stress	Addison's Disease	Masculinizes boys and women
	Androgen	Assists in sexual development	Retardation or lack of sexual development	Masculinity in females; unknown in males
	Estrogen	Assists in sexual development	Retardation or lack of sexual development	Femininity in males; upsets menstrual cycle in females

GLAND	HORMONES	FUNCTIONS	DEFICIENCY	EXCESS
Gonads:				
Ovaries	Estrogen	Female secondary sexual characteristics; stimulates reproductive organs to develop	Retardation of sexual development	Unknown
	Progesterone	Development of uterus in preparation for pregnancy	Miscarriage of early embryo	Unknown
Testes	Testosterone (Androgen)	Male secondary sexual characteristics; stimulates reproductive organs to develop	Retardation of sexual development	Unknown
Placenta	Placental Gonadotrophin (embryonic portions)	Suppresses production of gonadotrophin, thereby preventing further ovulation	Unknown	Unknown
	Estrogen	Seems to counteract effect of LTH upon mammary glands, preventing milk formation	Unknown	Unknown
	Progesterone	Takes over function of corpus luteum progesterone as it diminishes	Miscarriage of fetus	Unknown

FAMILIES AS SOCIALIZERS

When a child is born, he's born not only into a family but into a society. Each society has different rules and expectations for how they think their members should act. A child does not know these expectations when he is born, and so he has to be taught them as he is growing up. Anciently, the only socializing influence on a child was the family-- usually the extended family. A child had parents, aunts, uncles, cousins, and grandparents all living in close proximity. They taught the child the rules of the family and how to work and cooperate. There were no schools or government policies or mass media presentations. The bulk of a child's time was spent with family members who socialized him. As the family became more nuclear and moved away from close contact with siblings and parents, other socializing agents came into existence.

In figure 1 we have listed several major socializing agents: family, friends, church, school, the media, government policies, and cultural heritage. We want you to evaluate each of these socializers as to how much control a parent can have over them. Put down a score of "0" if you think a parent has no control, a "1" if a parent has some control, and a "2" if a parent can have total control over each of them. The reason you are doing this is because today's parents know their children are going to be exposed to messages and lifestyles different from what they teach in the home and they panic. But if parents can control some of the other message their children hear, they won't have to be as nervous. Parenting can be grim when you feel you have no control over the impact other people or institutions have on your children.

FIGURE 1

Family	_____
Friends	_____
School	_____
Church	_____
TV	_____
Magazine	_____
Government	_____
Cultural heritage	_____

0 = no control   1 = some control   2 = total control

Now that you've made your judgement, let us tell you what can happen. You can have near total control over the family. A husband and wife should be able to send a unified message to their children regarding values and so on. It's possible to have total control over the church you belong to, not by altering the church, but by finding a church that teaches the same things you do. Similarly, you can have great control over the school, not by telling teachers what to teach, but by finding a school that teaches and reinforces the things that you do. To find such a school might mean your children would go to a private school. The ultimate private school--one that you would definitely have total control over-- would be a home school. There are thousands of families who teach their children at home, especially through the elementary school years. In a home school, the parent has total control because they decide the curriculum, and pick out the texts and so on. Unless you are really into censoring things, you won't have much control over what your children are exposed to in the media (TV and magazines), nor can you control their friends. And you will have very little control over government policies. You don't have to be in control of all these socializers to have a happy life. If you can control just a few, then you are going to be able to raise great children wherever you live.

The impact of the family can be more important and powerful than any other socializer, especially in the long term. There may be short periods of time when friends will have more influence, but if you've bonded your children to you and you have a loving and nurturing home, then you're going to be the most powerful socializer. And remember, your family is the first social institution your child encounters. He who teaches first, teaches best.

Researchers have looked at many parental qualities to see what ones seem to make a difference in terms of how children turn out. They have sort of decided there are three qualities that account for most of the differences. The first is the amount of control a parent exerts over their children. It can vary from very little control--called autonomy --to total control. The second dimension is the amount of warmth parents show to children. It varies from aloof or hostile to loving. The third dimension is the amount of anxiety parents feel regarding their role as parents. It varies from high anxious (neurotic) to low anxious (calm). There are many reasons why a parent might have low control over their children: fear, so they don't make choices; anger, their children aren't worth spending time with; and trust, they believe their children are good inside and they let them choose. There are also several reasons why a person may feel high or low anxiety, or high or low warmth. Because there are several reasons for each state of mind, this model isn't perfect, but it can teach us some general truths. We have tried to visualize for you how these three dimensions interact. Look at figure 2. Picture that all parents can be represented by a round ball. We can divide the ball into a left part and a right part and let those parts represent hostile and warm parents respectively. Then we can divide the ball into a top part and a bottom part and let these parts represent autonomous (no control) parents and controlling parents respectively. Finally we can divide the ball into a front part and a back part and let those parts represent high anxiety and low anxiety (calm) parents respectively. The two circles in the figure represent the front and back parts (we can't draw in these dimensions). This creates eight different parental styles. We have labeled each one of them. A parent who is hostile, has low control, and is highly anxious is a rejecting parent. A parent who has low control but is warm, nurturant, and calm is a democratic parent. Parents don't divide equally into each of these eight types but there are families of each type. Each of these types describe family climates and different kinds of children that come from them. In figure 3 we've listed some of the characteristics of each family type and the children they produce.

In only two of these eight family climates do children thrive and become the very best that they can be. Children can usually learn to cope with any kind of a parental setting-- even a rejecting family or a dictatorial family--as long as that family is consistent in their behavior. Children learn to deal with abusive parents, so they don't psychologically wither up and die. But they don't reach their potential. The two types of family climates where children thrive are democratic and authoritative. Notice what is similar in those two family types. Both of these family types consist of parents who are calm, relaxed, and confident, and they both have parents that are warm and nurturant, and know how to express it.

It is in these two types of families where true bonding takes place. Bonding is an interesting phenomena. When children bond to their parents they identify with them, they want to be like them, and they adopt their value systems. So if you create a family that is loving and expressive, you are relaxed and enjoy being a parent. The odds are that you will have good children who will bond to you. This doesn't mean that parenting is going to be easy, but you will enjoy the hard work of being a parent and will enjoy your children. And you will have minimal worries about raising your children, no matter what other socializing voices your children may hear.

One belief that raises future parents' anxiety is that they can't be successful if they have a non-traditional family. The traditional family, which is diminishing year by year, consists of a father who works, a mother in the home, and a small number of children. Non-traditional families include single parent families and families with working mothers. Some people think that because they do not have a traditional family, that they are not good people. Good children are being raised in all types of families. There appear to be few differences in the children that come from families where mothers work and families where the mother is in the home. Good children come from both kinds of families and disturbed children come from both kinds of families. The important thing for a mother to realize if she decides to work is her attitude toward working. If a mother is happy with her work, then her attitude shows through in her parenting, and she will be relaxed and enjoy her children. To work outside of the home does not mean a mother has abandoned her children. Children actually benefit from good preschool experience where they interact with peers, as opposed to interacting with parents and brothers and sisters. They can learn things with peers, even at the age of two and three, that they cannot learn at home. There just aren't any more bad effects in children whose mothers work and are happy than in children whose mothers don't work and are happy, except that the former children tend to be a little more independent.

FIGURE 2

PARENT-CHILD INTERACTION MODEL
Wesley Becker (1964)

Three variables are used in the Parent-Child Interaction Model: support, control, and anxiety. By using these three variables, the following outcomes are possible.

    LC, LS, LA - Permissive   LC, LS, HA - Rejecting
    HC, LS, LA - Rigid Controlling   HC, LS, HA - Dictatorial
    LC, HS, LA - Democratic   LC, HS, HA - Overindulgent
    HC, HS, LA - Authoritative   HC, HS, HA - Overprotective

LC = Low Control, HC = High Control, LA = Low Anxiety, HA = High Anxiety, LS = Low Support, HS = High Support

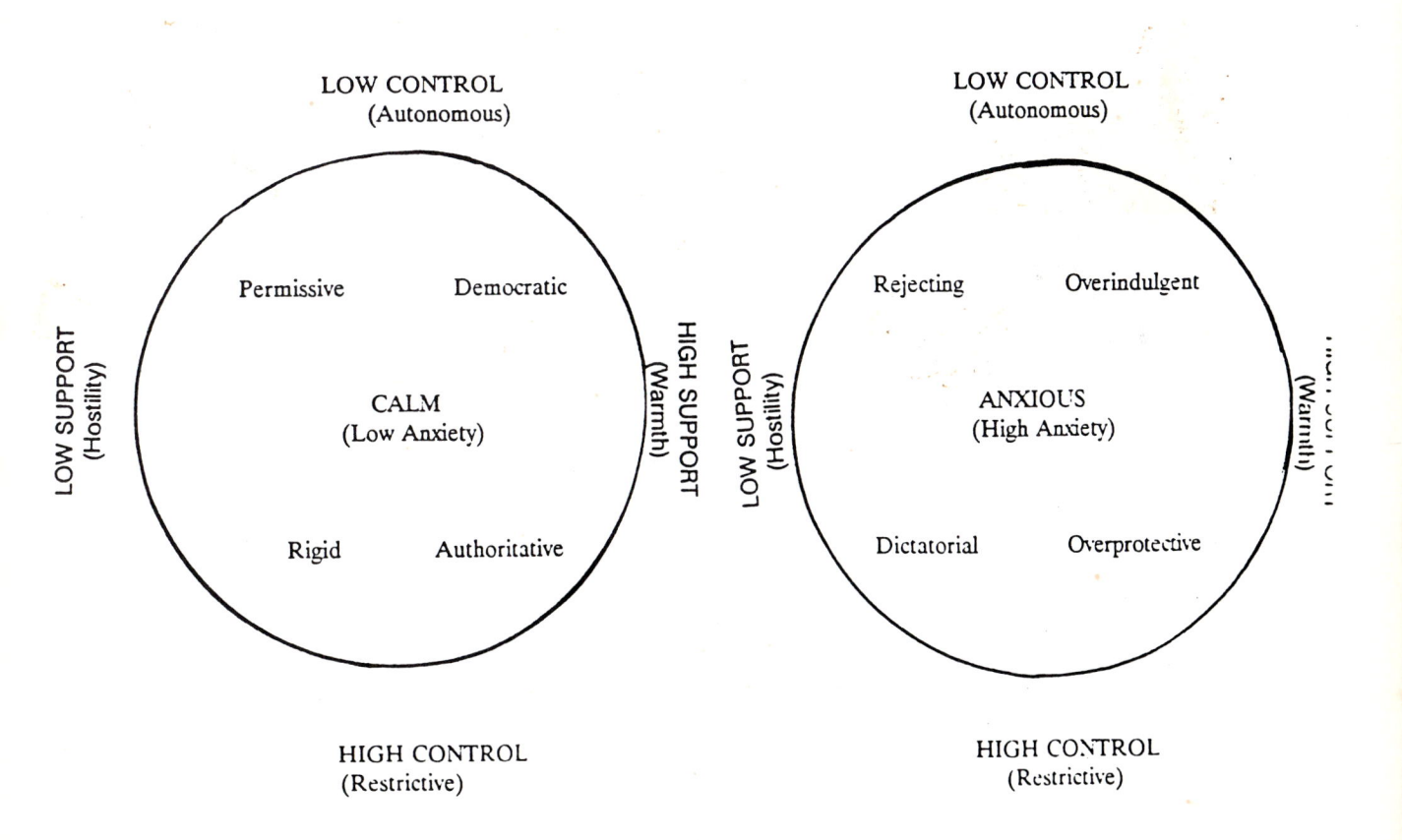

Left circle:

LOW CONTROL (Autonomous)

LOW SUPPORT (Hostility) — HIGH SUPPORT (Warmth)

- Permissive / Democratic
- CALM (Low Anxiety)
- Rigid / Authoritative

HIGH CONTROL (Restrictive)

Right circle:

LOW CONTROL (Autonomous)

LOW SUPPORT (Hostility) — (Warmth)

- Rejecting / Overindulgent
- ANXIOUS (High Anxiety)
- Dictatorial / Overprotective

HIGH CONTROL (Restrictive)

FIGURE 3

CHARACTERISTICS OF PARENTS & CHILDREN

Permissive (LC, LS, LA)

<u>Parents</u>   Self-centered, selfish, show lack of concern and lack of warmth, often highly inconsistent in their use of discipline
<u>Children</u>   Many delinquents come from this type of home, and generally display aggressive or uncontrolled behavior

Rigid Controlling (HC, LS, LA)

<u>Parents</u>   Restrictive and hostile, but do not allow the children to show hostility towards them
<u>Children</u>   Shy, socially withdrawn, anxious, neurotic, and self-punishing

Democratic (LC, HS, LA)

<u>Parents</u>   Warm and supportive, limits and rules set by parents AND children. The concept of a family council is often used. Show confidence in children and cooperate with them
<u>Children</u>   Creative and independent, socially outgoing, achievements are self-rewarding, moderately compliant, non-conformist. Also considered by some as rowdy, not submissive, lacking obedience

Authoritative (HC, HS, LA)

<u>Parents</u>   A few highly structured rules and limits established for the children's benefit, very methodical in decision making, high standards of excellence established (within reasonable limits), push children to function at peak of their abilities, and generally warm, confident, support, and success oriented
<u>Children</u>   Usually "model" children. They have a strong conscience, very compliant, and respect persons with authority over them

Rejecting (LC, LS, HA)

<u>Parents</u>   Feel the world is out to get them and see their children as the main source of their anxiety--children are a symbol of the parents' inability to cope with the real world
<u>Children</u>   Reflect parents' anxiety, motivated to perform antisocial behavior, socially punitive, and aggressive

Dictatorial (HC, LS, HA)

<u>Parents</u>   Highly restrictive, punitive, and similar to Rigid Controlling parents. They try to appease their anxiety by striking out at their children. The anxiety and frustration is caused by sources outside the family
<u>Children</u>   Like those of Rigid Controlling children

Overindulgent (LC, HS, HA)

<u>Parents</u>   They fear that they will frustrate their children, so they set no limitations or restrictions on them. Submit to all children's desires
<u>Children</u>   Extremely independent, manipulators, antisocially aggressive, little development of conscience which causes a lack of compliance and mischievousness

Overprotective (HC, HS, HA)

<u>Parents</u>   Lives centered completely around children, do not use physical punishment, use love withdrawal and emotional manipulation to control child, establish high standards of achievement, remove obstacles that might cause misbehavior
<u>Children</u>   Set unrealistic goals for themselves in an attempt to please parents, highly compliant and dependent on parents, strong conscience development in order to protect against parents' withdrawal of love

LEARNING ACTIVITY

Complete a copy of the following questionnaire yourself and then have your parents fill it out. Mark each item according to this scale: 1 - strongly disagree; 2 - disagree; 3 - agree; 4 - strongly agree. You should fill out one page and send the second to your parents to fill out. When they return it to you, transfer the information onto your sheet and compare.

YOUR SHEET

	Your Perception			Parents' Perception	
	You	Mom	Dad	Mom	Dad
1. I believe in a personal God					
2. My religious affiliation is the only right way					
3. The Democratic Party basically brings about needed change					
4. The Republican Party tries to preserve the Constitution					
5. America has a role to help the world					
6. America is always right in international affairs					
7. America is the best country					
8. I appreciate and value contracts with minority people					
9. The color of a man's skin should not affect my feelings towards him					
10. Violence is often necessary to bring about change					
11. The youth of today have generally had too little discipline and this has contributed to the disregard of the law					
12. All war is bad					
13. Some wars serve good purposes					
14. If you conscientiously object to a war, you shouldn't have to fight in it					
15. Society ought not to have laws regarding sexual matters between two consenting adults					
16. Youth who date should limit their affection to a half dozen good night kisses					
17. It is better to be an introvert than an extrovert					
18. A college education is the greatest goal a person can strive for					
19. A person should always do his best					
20. Most people who succeed do so because they have worked hard					
21. You have to be a little shifty and unethical to get ahead in this world					
22. Politicians really can't be honest					
23. A person should be honest no matter what					
24. Marijuana is worse than tobacco					

LEARNING ACTIVITY

PARENTS' SURVEY

Parents' Perception
Mom   Dad

1. I believe in a personal God
2. My religious affiliation is the only right way
3. The Democratic Party basically brings about needed change
4. The Republican Party tries to preserve the Constitution
5. America has a role to help the world
6. America is always right in international affairs
7. America is the best country
8. I appreciate and value contracts with minority people
9. The color of a man's skin should not affect my feelings towards him
10. Violence is often necessary to bring about change
11. The youth of today have generally had too little discipline and this has contributed to the disregard of the law
12. All war is bad
13. Some wars serve good purposes
14. If you conscientiously object to a war, you shouldn't have to fight in it
15. Society ought not to have laws regarding sexual matters between two consenting adults
16. Youth who date should limit their affection to a half dozen good night kisses
17. It is better to be an introvert than an extrovert
18. A college education is the greatest goal a person can strive for
19. A person should always do his best
20. Most people who succeed do so because they have worked hard
21. You have to be a little shifty and unethical to get ahead in this world
22. Politicians really can't be honest
23. A person should be honest no matter what
24. Marijuana is worse than tobacco

CHILD OBSERVATION

INTRODUCTION

The term socialization refers to the way children learn the rules, customs, and traditions of their culture. There are many factors which influence whether children become socialized or learn unsocialized behavior. Some of these factors are a child's family and friends, the media, schools, and the amount of exposure children have to positive or negative influences.

In this class project you are asked to do the following.

PART I

Get a spiral note book and lay it open. Label the left-hand page OBSERVATION OF CHILD. Divide the right-hand page vertically down the middle and label the two parts WHAT OTHER CHILDREN ARE DOING and INTERPRETATION OF BEHAVIOR. Observe a preschool child for 3 hours--1 hour a week for 3 weeks. Observe the same child each week. If that child is absent, observe another child. In the center section write a description of what the other children are doing at the same time. Then in the column on the right evaluate or interpret each observation. Indicate whether the behavior is an example of socialized behavior (e.g. following rules, adapting emotions, interacting successfully with other children, etc.) or if it is an example of unsocialized behavior. Then describe the <u>stage of play</u> the child was engaging in.

Observation of child	What other children are doing	Interpretation of behavior
Cuts paper very slowly - cuts blue paper. Puts it with other papers. Cuts yellow paper - tidys up work area. Starts cutting. "Hey Teacher! Look at this stuff!"	5 other kids are cutting paper - don't seem to be interacting at all	Parallel Play
A boy takes his scissors + he grabs them back. They push and shove. "You dummy! Give me my scissors!" "I don't have to - dummy!" Takes scissors and puts scissors up. Puts paper on shelf and goes outside and watches other kids play in mud.	Boy takes scissors. He is not one of the original cutters. Small fight.	Boy seems preoccupied with being neat.
A girl says, "Can you walk in the mud?" Boy says, "I want to be a duck." He walks in the mud and follows the girl as they splash around.	Boy seems excited to be invited to play in the mud. He imitates the girl.	Cooperative Play

Write down everything your child says and does under the observation column. Be specific and detailed. Also be objective. Let your eye be a camera and describe only what you see. Every 5 minutes leave a space so we can tell how much the child does in 5 minutes. You should have 4 to 6 inches of <u>normal</u> sized handwriting for each 5 minutes.

PART II

At the end of the notebook <u>write out</u> examples of six of the following.

1. Two children resolving a conflict. How mature was their solution?
2. Understanding the law of cause and effect.
3. Making a moral decision, and the level of moral reasoning the child uses.
4. Demonstrating ego-centric thought.
5. Realizing the difference between fantasy and reality.
6. Following or violating a social rule.
7. Helpful or hurtful behavior.
8. Cooperation.
9. Social passivity.
10. Regulation of emotion.
11. Adapting emotions.
12. Self-confidence.

If you haven't seen 6 of these in your observation, observe a fourth time and look at any child for examples.

PART III

After conducting your observations, write a 4-5 page paper. In this paper include the following:

1. The goal or objectives of healthy social development
2. How children acquire a self-concept and a concept of other people.
3. How children learn about and apply social rules.
4. How parents and families contribute to or distract from social development.
5. How problems in social development may be caused.

SELF-REGULATION

Self-regulation is the process by which an individual exerts some form of inner control to achieve a desired result when there are distractions, persuaders, or other influences that must be resisted to do so. It has also been called impulse control, deferred gratification, self-control, and resistance to temptation.

Self-regulation itself is an adoptive strategy which a person develops to control the amount of environmental pressure he feels. Humans make plans to act intentionally and appear to devise strategies that will help them carry out what is intended while they are in the association of others, while they are confronted with other attractive alternatives, and while motivational levels fluctuate.

There is some indication that this develops spontaneously. A child's awareness of his self-regulation strategies appears after eight years of age. For example, Mischel (1978) reported a study designed to identify how preschoolers, third graders, and sixth graders postpone pleasure. After age eight, children were significantly better able to identify their strategies than were the preschool children.

The development of self-regulation has been associated with the formation of inner speech. This internal dialogue appears to be a necessary part of forming strategies of self-control. The most detailed theory of self-regulation is described by Vygotsky (1962). He proposes that at first a child is regulated by an adult and learns the adult's language and style of thought. During the time this is taking place a child is highly influenced by the context in which a child performs. This means, for example, a child would pay more attention to a mother's instructions than to cues helping to solve a problem. As inner speech develops, a child's attention shifts from environmental cues to those inherent in solving a problem. The child therefore, becomes more self-regulated.

Vygotsky suggests that this development takes place in four steps. The first involves adult-child interactions when the child fails to correctly interpret the adult's speech resulting in failure to adequately regulate the child's performance. This evolves into a situation where the child more adequately comprehends adult speech and successfully performs because of the "other" regulation of the parent. The adult-child interaction, however, teaches the child to recognize the cues necessary to perform a task. The third level consists of the child making a transition from "other" to "self" regulation. The child senses the cues necessary to perform the task and performs them with some minimal interaction with the adult for reassurance. Level four is simply a further advancement to the point that a child performed the task, using inner thought to succeed at the task.

Based on Vygotsky's theory it appears possible to enhance this development by rehearsal and by effective adult involvement. Children could, for example, be helped to focus on the requirements of a task, encouraged to perform them, and evaluate his or her inner speech related to the task. Such activities help focus thoughts on what a child intended to do, thus minimizing the effects of distractions.

SEQUENCE OF DEVELOPMENT

Initial Comprehension
Age 0-3

A child has minimal understanding of his or her thoughts and also fails to accurately understand language meanings of other regulators.

Interaction
Age 4-7

Children more fully understand explanations, descriptions, rules, and suggestions of other regulations and participate in verbal discussions about tasks. This enables a child to more correctly sense the demands of a task and enables him to choose what must be done to successfully perform. This stage is characterized by indications that a child is beginning to defer gratification and develop impulse control.

Self-Regulation Assurance
Age 8-12

Children can now identify their strategies of self-regulation and adopt them or form new ones to fit different situations. Adapting them, however, involves checking for external/adult confirmation. One may see responses ranging from well-developed self-regulation to pronounced attempts to gain confirmation from others.

Self-Regulation
Ages 12-18

Children's adaptive strategies can be clearly observed as they successfully participate in varieties of activities. Self-regulation is made definite in the forms of impulse control, resistance to temptation, and self-control. Adolescents formulate plans to perform tasks and achieve more of them by using strategies of self-regulation.

LEARNING ACTIVITIES

I. Objective: To demonstrate the effectiveness of inner speech as a means of achieving self-regulation.

- A. Select something you wish you could stop doing, but are not always successful (e.g. eating unnecessary food).
- B. During a period of meditation, visualize yourself approaching the time and situation you wish to stop doing. Say in your mind, "Stop! Stop it!" Add any other strategy you wish to. Also see many "Stop" signs located in different places. Repeat once on each of four days.
- C. Answer the following questions:
  1. Why did you select to stop?
     _____
     _____

  2. Describe how you visualized the scene and the "inner speech" you used.
     _____
     _____

  3. Evaluate the results: What helped? What did not help?
     _____
     _____

II. Objective: To develop self-regulation strategies for different tasks.

- A. Select three of the following situations where you have the most difficult time performing as you would. Describe what you actually do in each and what you would prefer instead.
  1. Eating
     Actual   _____
     Preferred _____

  2. Communicating with _____.
     Actual   _____
     Preferred _____

  3. With friends
     Actual   _____
     Preferred _____

  4. With family
     Actual   _____
     Preferred _____

5. At work
   Actual _____
   Preferred _____

6. On a date
   Actual _____
   Preferred _____

B. Select from the following strategies the ones you think might work and use at least one to attempt to achieve the preferred behavior.
   1. Rehearse the new way of acting and role play with a friend.

   2. Identify the cues you respond to in a less effective way and say them aloud in the situation.

   3. Tie your preferred performance to a specific cue you can see happening in the situation. Do this by thinking repeatedly about it.

   4. Develop a plan of thought you can use to prevent you from responding in the old way.

   5. Write your goals and the results of trying to achieve them.

A PRACTICAL IDENTITY

The word "identity" may be somewhat vague to you and in some ways it is not easy to understand. Yet, as a practical part of life we all know many things about it and use this knowledge every day. For example, everyone can be identified by a name, religion, nationality, cultural background, career, and hobbies. "I am a teacher," "I am from Peru," "I am a Mormon," are examples of identity statements.

Identity is made up of the knowledge we possess about ourselves. This "self knowledge" exists when we become aware of our inherited abilities and characteristics such as height, weight, and other physical traits. In addition, we also acquire self-knowledge about ways we act, how we think, and what we think, and what we feel. A person, for example, could know about his/her intellectual abilities, emotional style, poor eyesight, and that he/she is loved, supported, or not loved and supported by others. An identity is formed when this information is first discovered and then integrated in some organized way. When this takes place, the result is fairly permanent. Identity is not a shirt we put on and take off when it is convenient or when we feel like it. Identity is the meaning found in the words we use to describe ourselves and others. We talk about identity when we say, "I am a happy person," or "she is very loving," or "I trust him because he is very honest."

The biological basis for identity exists in the structure of the brain which develops and organizes our thoughts and experiences. As we grow and mature our brains develop increased abilities to organize, synthesize, and integrate what we think, feel, and how we act. This is natural. All people go through the same process. This is similar to what happens when we put a jigsaw puzzle together. While the pieces are in the box we think and say its identity is "a puzzle." Even when we are putting the pieces together we think of it as a puzzle. But, when the very last piece is in, or integrated, we think of it as a picture of some kind. The integration of all the parts has made the puzzle into a new concept or identity.

THE IMPORTANCE OF IDENTITY

Identity is, at the same time, the most basic and far reaching idea in human behavior. It is related to virtually everything we do. Since it is all that we think about when we think about ourselves it comes into play in virtually every choice, every act, every relationship. Our religious belief or non beliefs, our values, our work behavior are all part of identity. It is motivation for performance and achievement. It is how we express ourselves as a married person, a parent, a friend.

Identity can also be understood from times when it is incomplete or not fully formed. Consider a child who has received frequent beatings from an overly harsh parent. These beatings take place whenever a parental rule has not been followed or when the parent acts without concern for the child. Since the beatings cause pain, the child begins to be afraid whenever there is concern about parental disapproval. What may happen as this child matures? It is possible that he will be more interested in avoiding the disapproval of others than becoming aware about himself and expressing his identity accurately. Like this child, limited self-knowledge prevents us from forming a complete sense of identity.

There are several conditions which prevent self-knowledge from emerging in us. These may include excessive dependency between parent and child, emotional neglect from parents to children, early trauma, and enmeshment a condition where a child is not permitted to form a sense of unique individuality. When one or more than one of these conditions exist a developing child is prevented from acquiring self-knowledge. The pieces of his/her life puzzle cannot be put together and the formation of identity is incomplete.

SIGNS OF COMPLETE AND INCOMPLETE IDENTITY FORMATION

There are many indications when one's identity is completely formed as well as when it is not. Many of life's problems are evidenced when one's sense of identity is weak and life's successes exist when identity is strong.

Complete Identity Formation	Incomplete Identity Formation
more productive	less productive
strong sense of self-control	depression
satisfying relationships	unstable in relationships
more positive emotions	more anxiety and anger
accept responsibility	assume too much guilt
assertive	"walked on by others"
	inhibition

HOW TO MAINTAIN IDENTITY

The pressures of life's routine and involvements we have in work, church and play can weaken one's sense of identity. In order to feel secure and confident about what we do it is necessary to learn maintenance skills which enable us to perpetuate a strong sense of identity. One of these is a sense of self-control. This is maintained by awareness that we make choices which we act out and are responsible for. Therefore, to maintain identity we need to have a procedure for making choices and then accepting the results of our actions without blaming or criticizing anyone else for what happens. Secondly, identity is maintained by a condition of separation. This means that instead of linking ourselves to others by suggesting they cause what we think, feel, or do we need to attribute the cause of what we are to ourselves. This will sound like, "I do this because of what I think or feel," or "I think this because of what I feel," or "I feel because I think." This separating our thoughts from the acts of other people will remove the false links we establish between us and other people. Third, maintaining a strong sense of identity is accomplished when we learn to be expressive. That is, to say what we think or feel in many different situations. When we are expressive we feel freer and more positive than when we cannot speak about our own thoughts and feelings.

Imagine yourself on a date, in a conversation with parents, talking with a church authority, deciding what to do with a friend, in an argument with a brother or sister. In which of these situations are you most likely to blame, feel your behavior is caused by someone, or see yourself as inhibited. Your answers will tell you the situation(s) where you have the easiest and hardest time maintaining your sense of identity.

LEARNING ACTIVITY

Objective: To help you learn what identity is, when it is complete or incomplete and how to maintain it.

1. How many of the items under Complete Identity apply to you?
   _____
   _____
   _____

2. How many of the items under Incomplete Identity apply to you?
   _____
   _____
   _____

3. Describe your typical behavior in the following situations.

   a. with a member of the opposite sex who is a romantic interest.
      _____
      _____
      _____

   b. with a same sex friend._____
      _____
      _____

   c. when someone is telling you what to do._____
      _____
      _____

   d. when you are in charge of or supervise other people._____
      _____
      _____

   e. when you have to perform in public._____
      _____
      _____

4. From your descriptions above, identify those you are able to feel a strong sense of self-control and are freely expressive of your thoughts and feelings._____
   _____
   _____
   _____

5. Describe at least two events or experiences which prevented you from feeling a strong sense of identity._____
_____
_____
_____
_____

6. Write a plan of at least six steps designed to help you strengthen your sense of identity. Consider:
   a. achievement
   b. service (social interest)
   c. love (giving and receiving)
   d. increasing your social network

IDENTITY FORMATION

Begun when children are very young and elaborated as they mature, the sense of individuality we call identity is more fully realized during the latter parts of adolescence and early adulthood. Identity formation within human beings is a combination of many things. Among these are the following: (1) goals and the ability to organize to reach them, (2) stable values and the ability to decide what is or is not consistent with them, (3) having appropriate understanding of important social roles (e.g. husband, friend, wife, and etc.), (4) self regulation, and (5) a capacity for fun and enjoyment.

Individuals develop these characteristics at varying rates, but there is some evidence (Montemayor & Eisen, 1977) that all development follows some clearly discernable trends. These authors asked children of different ages to respond to the question "Who am I?". Younger children answered by associating themselves with places, other people, and physical characteristics. The older the children surveyed, the more likely it is that they think of themselves in more abstract ways (e.g. "I am a lover," or "I am a human being"). We can conclude from this report that much of the formation of identity is due to maturation of body and brain. Like nearly all other areas of development, however, a positive identity also is due to conditions in one's environment. These conditions appear to be actual achievement, self-awareness, and self regulation. A person could be said to use abstract thinking, achievements, knowledge about himself, and the confidence acquired from self control to organize attitudes which comprise the larger concept of identity. An individual who does not achieve, or has little self awareness and/or who fails to regulate his behavior would have difficulty achieving a sense of identity.

Of interest to us, however, is the unique way an individual uses abstract thought to integrate maturational and environmental influences. During late adolescence, it seems the major activity in identity formation is the synthesizing of several parts of one's personality. One person may use his/her achievement more prominently in the way identity is expressed while another may use some other aspect.

It seems clear though, that identity depends on an individual finding ways to see relationships between many characteristics which heretofore have been separate. These relationships may be similar to recognizing how one thinks or feels about many different people or situations and concludes that "I am generally optimistic," or "I think things over carefully before I decide." Adolescence may be characterized as the time when an individual integrates and develops a sense of "wholeness" about himself.

Anyone wishing to contribute to the formation of another's identity can do so by helping him or her first achieve self awareness and develop self control. Then activities, which include conversations and decision making, (which requires a synthesis of personality characteristics) can be used to promote an integration of this condition into a fairly stable sense of identity.

DEVELOPMENT OF IDENTITY

	ENVIRONMENT	**MATURATION**
Individual Status, Age 0-3	Learns and relates to a name. Acquires knowledge about the world and begins to adapt to people and the uses of objects.	Development of senses, physical abilities, earliest sex-roles adjustment. Achieves physical skills of eating, toilet training, running, walking, skipping.
Social Status, Age 3-7	The adaptation to varieties of social situations promotes self-knowledge in fairly concrete ways. "I can now run fast...I am big!" These self-references are used as explanations for social status.	Begins to use physical abilities as a primary way of relating to other people. Social status is based on how skillful or unskillful a child may be.
Achievement, Age 7-12	Children develop levels of achievement motivation and use them in various tasks. These may include academic work, specialized talents, and/or chores at home. The ability to utilize self-regulation comes into play in order to balance achievement activities with other experiences: Achievement becomes more specialized and individuals begin to better recognize what they might successfully achieve	Cognitive maturation allows the emotional control necessary in achievement behavior. Increased mental growth also permits more focused introspection that results in greater awareness of one's attitudes, motives, and moods.
Identity Formation, Age 13-	Increased social involvement promotes more awareness and self-consciousness. Achievements can be recognized by important groups and used to achieve status.	Children evidence an improved ability to think abstractly which permits them to perceive relationships among their own personality traits. These relationships are formed into the generalized beliefs that make up the concept of identity.

LEARNING ACTIVITIES

I. Recognize the characteristics of achievements, self-knowledge, and self-control.

   Purpose: To help students more clearly recognize their experience in each of the three learned identity areas.

   1. Write a description of your social and personal achievements. This may include such things as work, academics, talent development, social positions held, and levels of popularity.

   2. Describe your emotional style in the following situations. Include (a) what feelings or attitudes you actually experience, and (b) how rapidly or slowly you come to recognize these feelings.
      a. starting something new
      b. being criticized by someone in authority
      c. having done something wrong
      d. when you have to make a difficult decision
      e. when you are neglected by someone
      f. when you have succeeded at something and when you have failed

   3. Describe the areas in which you exhibit the greatest and the least self-discipline and give examples to show how you do it.

   4. Evaluate your ability to regulate yourself.

II. Integrating personal characteristics into alternatives for future choices.

   Purpose: To promote the integration of students' personality characteristics.

   1. Based on what you know about your ability to achieve, to understand your thoughts and feelings, and to regulate yourself, estimate your chances of succeeding at the following and give an explanation for your estimate.
      a. parenthood
      b. a college degree
      c. someone recognized as an honest person
      d. a career in medicine
      e. a career in business
      f. a career in education
      g. becoming wealthy
      h. being religious
      i. making a significant contribution to society
      j. having the ability to establish satisfying heterosexual relationships

2. Ask five people to respond to the foregoing list of ten items and estimate their chances of succeeding. Record their answers and examine whether the individuals base their estimate on their perceived ability to achieve, to understand themselves, and/or to regulate themselves.

Answer the following questions:

a. Do people use a similar or unique style of thinking about their future?

b. In what ways are people the same and in what ways did they differ in formulating a rationale for their estimation?

III. Write a paper which describes how identity is achieved and what prevents it. Hand in results of all surveys and your answers to questions.

THE DEVELOPMENT OF INDEPENDENCE

Independence is a general concept widely used to describe a child's separation from parents, but there is little agreement about what it means specifically. It is usually viewed as financial self-sufficiency and in more abstract terms of emotional or psychological separation. Achieving it is viewed as a major developmental task of adolescence because dependence, the opposite of independence, is an indication of limited maturity.

The more children are independent the more likely they are to make individual decisions, feel able to rely on themselves for survival, and believe their efforts have reasonable chances of succeeding; further, independent people are, according to Erikson's stages of development, better able to establish intimate relationships. The relationship of independent children to parents is one of equality and mutual respect. Children acknowledge the parents' position by deferring occasionally to parental involvement and parents show respect by seldom advising or otherwise intruding in their children's lives. Parents and independent children are able to strike a positive balance between affection and individuality.

HOW ADOLESCENTS ACHIEVE INDEPENDENCE

Of the attempts to study how adolescents achieve independence, one stands out as especially significant. Daniel and Janet Offer collected information about these subjects over an eight year period. Results from the study were examined and showed three avenues of achieving. These types of development were characterized by: (1) continuous growth (23 percent of the total group), (2) surgent growth (35 percent of the total group), and (3) tumultuous growth (21 percent of the total group).

Those who experienced <u>continuous growth</u> were reported to cope well with internal and external stimuli and had mastered previous developmental stages without serious problems. Their parents grew and changed with the children. There was open expression of affection between parents and children during the eight years and capacity was exhibited to delay gratification and work for a future goal. Further, children expressed emotions but seldom let the expression get out of control.

Individuals who were in the group of <u>surgent growth</u> were those who appeared to experience rapid personality change and achieve independence in a short time period. These individuals showed reasonable coping behavior, but when a crisis arose, they tended to become angry and blame others. Consequently, relationships between adolescents and parents were not smooth. Furthermore, the parents of these individuals evidenced conflict between their basic values. These subjects were not as action oriented as the first group and were late in developing heterosexual interests. These individuals were less able to introspect than the others and evidenced constricted emotional responses.

Individuals who experienced <u>tumultuous growth</u> came from less favorable backgrounds than individuals in the other two groups. Many parents had open marital conflict, and others had a history of mental illness. Parents appeared to be unsure of their values and failed to resent a clearly defined set of values to their children. Both parents and children had difficulty separating from one another and their relationship was marked by great emotional intensity. Independence was achieved after years of instability and conflict.

The results of this study show that at least three avenues of independence exist. Further, we can see the close tie between the course of independence and a child's background. When we consider that mental and physical development are antecedents to independence, we can begin to recognize the complexity involved.

HOW TO PROMOTE INDEPENDENCE

Being independent is considered important by our culture. Because it is, those who achieve it benefit from the reinforcement and respect given by others. Those who have difficulty achieving independence from parents receive less admiration. Those involved with children, who hope for their success, can contribute by knowing how to help them prepare for increased independence.

In previous sections of this chapter, we have already read how independence is promoted when children have a stable family and positive relationship with parents. Beyond this, however, there are more specific things which promote it. One of these is ensuring that children, while young, have work of their own to perform and learn to do it responsibly.

Early development of achievement and a sense of responsibility for tasks is usually formed when children have regular household chores to perform or other outside activities like paper routes or achievement in school and/or sports.

Further, as children mature they can be helped to become more independent by being helped to make and carry out decisions they make about their own activities. One set of parents asked their children to participate in making decisions about homework, curfew time, and chores. Further, the parents frequently asked their children's opinions about values and current affairs.

When the children's opinions differed markedly from the parents, further conversations were invited. This joint participation was marked by encouragement from the parents. Plans about children's future activities away from home (work or school) were also talked about. Achieving independence seemed natural and appropriate.

Another set of parents decided their children could be independent by age eighteen. Working backwards from that time they selected several events that children would do in gradual stages and specified awards for doing them. They worked out a contract with their children and reported that children responded well to their plan.

The many different circumstances of life for young adults make the setting of the same effective procedures impossible for each person. It is likely better to understand some principles and guidelines and then apply them to children in an individual way. Some increased freedom from gradually reduced controls, well defined values, positive support, and a history of responsible achievement appear to be the ingredients necessary to achieve independence from parents.

DEVELOPMENT OF INDEPENDENCE

Sense of Self Age 0-11	Children emerge as individuals by developing age adequate language, physical cognitive, and social skills. A sense of self happens through early achievement, social experiences, and participation in family interaction.

Controlled Age 12-15	Membership in peer groups and greater social involvement Separation permits children to explore a wider range of experiences within a relatively secure environment. Children begin to exhibit "negative compliance" or opposition to the rules of values of authority figures. Mild negative compliance is usually viewed as a more positive predictor of independence. Extreme opposition, passively or aggressively, indicates a lack of progress toward independence.
Individuation Age 16-22	Children further refine individual opinions, values, and behavioral standards usually similar to their parents. Children may apply them in highly unique ways. Authority figures lose much of their image as rule givers and are viewed by children more realistically possessing ordinary human characteristics. Children also have developed future plans and are progressing toward them.

LEARNING ACTIVITY

Determining your level of Independence

Purpose: To enable students to identify the amount of independence achieved in several personality areas.

I. Fill out the chart below to identify the amount of independence you have now achieved. Answer the following questions:

Achievements	(1) Successfully achieved (2) Not yet achieved	How Accomplished or decided: Self=1; w/others=2; by others=3
Selected a Mate		
Selected a career		
Financial self-sufficiency		
Positive Relationship with Parents		
Well-defined values about religion		
Able to Achieve your own goals		
Date several people or select a variety of people as friends		

II. Write a two page paper describing the difference between dependent people and people with a strong sense of independence.

DATING AND COURTSHIP

Dating and courtship are the terms our society uses to describe the way adolescents become acquainted with heterosexual partners and establish an intimate bond. What people actually do to accomplish this is usually determined by the culture in which they have lived and grown. In the United States, young people generally engage in courtship with more freedom to choose partners and activities than youth in Far Eastern countries whose parents often select the partners and choose the courtship activities.

Although the patterns of dating and courtship are strongly influenced by an individual's cultural heritage, they are approached by young people in a developmental way. There appear to be some phases of dating and courting that are gradually entered into and which progress toward the culminating intimate relationship. Knowledge of these stages of growth enable us to consider what might be done to influence and improve the quality of this important social experience.

Early adolescents (recognizing considerable individual variation) usually begin to associate with members of the other sex for the purposes of being like by others, acquiring a sense of self-esteem from the social contact, and to participate with peers in group activities. Dating at this time takes the form of heterosexual group activities that take place in a "friendship" atmosphere. "Hanging out" at a popular cafe or other setting is a frequent pastime for adolescents who are entering into dating and courting relationships. These situations tend to be more relaxed and are more comfortable because they put less pressure on youth to participate in the emotional complexity of a two person relationship. These group contacts serve the purpose of teaching adolescents about how to meet other people, how to talk, and the general procedure of carrying out a "date."

When two person dating begins at about 14-17 years of age, adolescents enter into a period of mixed accomplishments. In the earlier parts of this period, dating takes place for the purpose of achieving or maintaining popularity. This dating reinforces dome behavior which may not be linked to the emotional qualities of a good spouse or a good partner. The best dates, according to the adolescents, are often those who can talk freely and keep things going, usually at a superficial level. Further, since dating is an indicator of popularity, not being involved is viewed as so negative that adolescents develop manipulative interpersonal games that are contrary to the formation of a more genuine intimacy.

Following this second phase of dating and courtship process, adolescents begin to date as a means of learning about one another and to find enjoyable heterosexual companionship. This motion leads to a more authentic and emotionally intense relationship that leads some to marriage. Others go through the pangs of fluctuating involvements eventually going on to other experiences.

The last phase of dating and courtship is more properly courting because its purpose is mate selection. Individuals date and enter into relationships to find compatibility leading to marriage. Lengthy conversations and a variety of explorations serve the purpose of revealing information that serves the purpose of deciding on a mate.

APPLYING WHAT WE KNOW ABOUT DATING AND COURTSHIP

There are at least two ways we can apply what we know about dating and courtship. One is to evaluate ourselves and our abilities according to the developmental phases described in the foregoing section. Another application is in the preparation of adolescents who are about to experience or who are currently involved in the dating process. Accurate information can help us make choices that contribute to our success.

When you evaluate yourself you can examine your recent dating experiences to find the phase or stage you are currently involved in. You can also identify your level of personal dating skills you have developed to this point and see if you are preparing yourself to progress.

You might also prepare yourself to use the information about dating and courtship to help others make good choices about what they can do to have enjoyable dating experiences. Your future children, your friends, or your younger brothers and sisters might be helped by what you can tell them.

DEVELOPMENTAL STAGES FOR DATING AND COURTSHIP

Early Adolescence:
<u>Getting Acquainted</u>

Adolescents form groups of heterosexual friends. These groups meet at school, church, or a favorite community location (e.g., drive-in cafe) to talk and learn the preliminary dating skills.

Middle Adolescence:
<u>Dating for Status</u>

Dating begins and is often for the purpose of maintaining social status or to achieve a certain level of popularity with same sex friends. Dating is often accompanied by superficial forms of interpersonal behavior. These may include attempts at sexual exploitation.

Middle to Late Adolescence:
<u>Dating for Companionship</u>

Increased social and personal confidence allows progress toward selecting people to date that provide enjoyment and satisfying companionship. Individuals communicate more authentically and attempts are made to identify mutual interests. Individuals now have enough knowledge to observe and evaluate their personality characteristics and those of their companions.

Late Adolescent to Adulthood:
<u>Mate Selection</u>

Dating loses some of its early casualness and becomes the method of exploring for and selecting a marriage partner. Interpersonal skills are refined and used to gather information enabling individuals to decide whether or not to marry. The style of communication includes many personal references and mutual evaluations of interpersonal dynamics.

LEARNING ACTIVITIES

Activity I: **Evaluation**

Purpose: To identify your dating skills and help select areas for improvement.

Answer true or false to each of the following statements:

___ 1. I am able to introduce myself to someone I would like to know without feeling uncomfortable.

___ 2. While I am on a date, I can easily participate in conversations without feeling hesitant.

___ 3. I am comfortable sharing personal opinions and experiences instead of feeling tongue-tied or superficial.

___ 4. I know how to make myself attractive to someone from the other sex and do not worry much about whether they will be interested in me.

___ 5. I am able to get second dates with those I would like to be with.

___ 6. I know the type of person I enjoy going on a date with and am not dating to find out what I prefer.

___ 7. I have a clear idea about the characteristics of someone I would like to marry or have a deeper relationship with.

___ 8. I listen attentively and often can show that I understand other people. I am not involved in conversation to clear up misunderstanding.

___ 9. I am comfortable maintaining my standards and beliefs when they are being compromised by someone.

___ 10. I enjoy sitting and talking with a date as much as I enjoy doing something else.

___ 11. I am interested in dating a variety of different people and do not want to be too involved with any one person.

___ 12. I prefer to date one person over a longer period of time and do not wish to do much casual dating.

KEY: As a general indication of your dating skills give yourself 1 point for each true answer on items 1-10. The higher the score, the more skillful you probably are (you might also give this test to someone you are dating). If you answered true to item 11, then you are probably not ready for a true courtship experience. If you answered true to item 12, you might be.

Activity II: **Preparation for Successful Dating**

Purpose: To gather information about the characteristics of people who have enjoyed successful dating experiences.

Note: There are two definitions of successful dating. One is the amount of interest and fun that people have. The second is whether dating has led to a more intimate relationship and marriage.

1. Interview six members of the other sex (3 who are older than 18 years of age and 3 who are younger than 18), and ask them to complete the following questions and the ranking tests.
    a. What are the 2 most prominent traits of someone you like to go out with (attractiveness, ability to talk, etc.)
    b. Describe the girl/guy with whom you have had the most fun on a date.
    c. Rank order the following list of personality traits in terms of what you prefer in someone you date.
        ___ sexual attractiveness
        ___ good conversationalist
        ___ honest
        ___ attentive
        ___ sensitive and aware of your feelings
        ___ affectionate
        ___ good sense of humor
        ___ interested in many different things

2. After you have collected the information from all six people, answer the following questions.
    a. Was there more agreement among the six people or more individual preferences? What conclusions would you form about the amount of agreement?
    b. How did the answers of the younger people differ from those of the older?

Activity III: Write a paper summarizing the results of "evaluation" and "preparation" activities.

DELINQUENCY

An individual is labeled delinquent because development has not or is not taking place toward the conventional values of society. Such delinquency is usually indicated by the expression of behavior considered deviant by those who follow society's rules.

Individuals who perform deviant acts and betray the values of society and/or family have developed this behavior much like development which takes place in other personality areas. Delinquent individuals include those who merely experiment with acts like shoplifting, drug usage or deception, as well as those who participate with peer groups in more regular deviant acts.

A careful analysis suggests that deviant actions symbolize the areas of growth that have not taken place. Sometimes we focus so much attention of finding ways to prevent deviance that we fail to consider an equally important idea. What prevents or hinders positive or conventional development from taking place? A consideration of this question may lead us to understand that delinquency, like positive growth, has its own developmental characteristics.

The roots of delinquency, for example, are probably related to any delay of ordinary development. Late physical development may be a factor. Social isolation of one or more forms may also contribute. Parental neglect, which may hinder social development, and parental overprotection, which hinders growth of a sense of responsibility may also be involved. A child's own temperament which affects his/her children, however, pose the more minor problem of social difficulty and/or experiment with deviant acts. These children usually make friends who are similar in their values and level of maturity. These friendships often exert such great influence that parents and other authorities find themselves in a position weakened by peer pressure. Sometimes children cannot be influenced and delinquent behavior runs the full course until some external influence or maturity helps them live more closely to the conventional rules of society.

When delinquent children are influenced toward increased maturity, it is largely because the underlying reasons for the behavior have been identified and responded to correctly. A child, for example, may be delinquent in developing because of some emotional trauma related to a parental divorce, death, or other social experience. In this case, resolution of the unfulfilled emotional need through discussion and love may be required. Other children may be delinquent because of a slow maturation rate. These children require guidance, support, and patience. Other children become caught in the web of environmental events and in order to grow must change their circumstances or be removed from them. The best strategy, however, is to not overreact, but accumulate as much information as possible about the child and then choose a course of action based on the reasons for the delinquent behavior.

THE DEVELOPMENT OF DELINQUENCY

The Diminished Self
0-10

Children, by virtue of neglect, overprotection, emotional enmeshment, delayed maturation, and/or abuse are prevented from developing a strong sense of individuality. They may manifest dependent behavior on parents, extreme temperament shifts, learning disorders, and/or problems relating to friends

Experimental
11-13

Delinquent children begin to experiment with and engage in activities which are precisely opposite of those desired by authority figures (e.g. if parents want the child to succeed in school he/she will fail). This is called negative compliance. Children show a greater tendency to lie and deceive as a means of creating a sense of increased freedom. This is an illusion. Experiments with deviant acts usually involve sensual activities such as use of drugs, alcohol, or sexual experiences.

Delinquent Peer Groups
14-older

Delinquent children join with other delinquent children and participate in deviant acts as a group. Group membership supports the children against guilt and/or pressure placed on them by authority figures. Group activities become central to their thinking and participation in deviant experiences is a requirement for membership. Values about personal responsibility, relationship to authority, and religious beliefs are mirrored among group members.

LEARNING ACTIVITIES

Activity I: **Normal Adolescent Development**

Purpose: To enable students to gather information about the type of activities considered a normal part of adolescence.

Instructions: Show the following survey to eight people (four male and four female). Ask them to indicate which of the activities they considered to be part of normal adolescent development. Answer the survey yourself before you administer it to others.

SURVEY

Listed below are some types of behavior that may or may not be a part of normal adolescent experience. Indicate your opinion by placing an 'X' in the square which reflects your belief.

	A part of Normal Adolescence	About half do it as part of growing up for nearly everyone	Rarely a part of anyone's adolescence
1. Petting with someone of the other sex			
2. Experimenting with drugs			
3. Drinking alcoholic beverages			
4. Violating traffic laws			
5. Shoplifting			
6. Conflict with parents			
7. Dressing in extreme styles			
8. Lying			
9. Destroying someone else's property			
10. Swearing and use of vulgar language			

a. How do the opinions of those you surveyed compare to yours?
b. Do males and females have different opinions about "normal adolescence?"
c. Do you think deviance is directed toward the values of others or directed toward the one who does deviant things? Support you answer from the data obtained from the survey.
d. Do the results from the survey reflect the values of our society or just those of the age group you surveyed?

Activity II: **The Positive Alternative**

Purpose: To help students identify what measures can be taken to help prevent the development of delinquent children.

Instructions: Write an evaluation of the following "parent principles" to see if they will or will not promote positive child development instead of delinquency. Support your opinion by showing how their application might affect children's lives.

1. Don't do for children what they can do for themselves.

2. Say what to do, instead of what not to do.

3. Spare the rod and spoil the child.

4. Don't push children; they will grow up just fine by themselves.

5. I am going to treat my children like my parents treated me.

6. All children need is to be loved.

7. If the parents agree, the family will be together.

SEX ROLES

Sex roles pervade every aspect of life. In every culture men and women have different duties, responsibilities, chores, and tasks. Sex roles are the socially prescribed ways a culture defines for the different genders to act. Since there are vast differences in the sex roles that societies assign their members, we know that sex roles are learned and not inherent in the nature of maleness or femaleness.

Gender typing--the awareness of one's gender--occurs in the early preschool years. It seems to involve two processes. First there is the process of learning which gender a person is and, second, learning what a person of that gender is supposed to do. As children begin to comprehend themselves and their world, one of the first things they understand, or concepts they form, is their own gender. They identify themselves as male or female and begin to organize their roles on the basis of that awareness. Once a child's understanding of his gender is firmly established--that is, a boy knows that he is a boy--they begin to use members of their own sex as models for their behavior. They form concepts of what boys or girls should be like. Then their concepts broaden and stretch as a boy assimilates his experiences of many boys. For instance, he realizes that short hair does not necessarily mean that someone is a boy, as he comes in contact with boys and men who have long hair and women who have short hair.

Eventually the child's own self-concept becomes assimilated into his concept of gender; I am a male, thus the qualities I possess are qualities of maleness. At this point children have a feedback loop. They compare their behaviors and actions with their concepts of maleness or femaleness, and then they evaluate themselves. This acts as a motivation to help them conform their behaviors to the concept of their gender that they have developed.

Parents play an important role in helping a child develop a concept of gender. In families where parents have traditional views of male and female roles, a child will also develop that same concept.

An interesting topic in developmental psychology today is the question of whether there should be specific gender roles for men and women. Sandra Bem has suggested that human behaviors and personality attributes should not be linked to gender. Instead of the stereotypical notions of masculinity and femininity, a concept has evolved of androgyny. An androgynous person is one who describes himself with both traditionally masculine adjectives and traditionally feminine adjectives. Since androgynous people score high in both masculine and feminine kinds of traits we might expect them to be the optimal functioning human beings. Indeed some research has shown that people with a high self-esteem are those who score high on an androgynous test. Androgynous people are very flexible in their roles and can adapt to whatever role their present life demands. They do not see the world in terms of specific tasks assigned to men and women but a blending of tasks of shared responsibility.

In college Preparation for Marriage classes, the vast majority of students claim they would like to have a companionate marriage--that is, one where both partners share jobs equally. Sometimes the wife cooks and cleans up, and sometimes the husband. Sometimes the husband takes care of the children, and sometimes the wife. The distribution of duties is determined by the individual needs and free time of each individual partner. The kind of personality that lends itself most ideally to a companionate marriage is the androgynous personality.

It should be noted that a marriage between two androgenous people is not the only successful kind of marriage. An excellent marriage can be made between a very traditional masculine male and feminine female because there is a clear understanding of the roles of each partner.

Androgynous people differ from traditionally masculine and feminine people in their beliefs about the differences between the sexes. Androgenous people see very little different psychological differences between the sexes. They see that there are more intra-sex differences on any psychological trait than there are inter-sex differences. The trend among college age students seems to be towards an equality and a fuzzing of the lines between male and female roles.

Given the barrage of gender-related information that children encounter on television, in advertising, and with toys, how can a parent help a child to develop an androgynous personality? One way is for parents to make gender irrelevant in the home.

Activities such as who cooks and does dishes, what toys are available, what games children can play, and what roles children can pick when they play house should not be determined by a child's sex. When their children are young parents can select books and television programs which teach children that one's sex is mostly a matter of anatomical differences and reproductive traits and not much else. They can point out examples of members of both sexes doing wide varieties of tasks and being happy, content, and fulfilled in doing them.

When androgynous college men were asked about their families, they said that their fathers had been highly involved in their lives, and that they felt close to their mothers. Similarly, androgenous women tended to be close to their fathers and had mothers who modeled and encouraged achievement in intellectual pursuits, curiosity, and doing well in school.

It is unlikely that society will abolish or reverse gender roles totally. This is sad in some ways because many obstacles to the advancement of women are based upon the prejudices or preconceived notions that others have of what women should do.

At the end of this chapter is a test on androgyny. You are to give yourself a score on each of the sixty items. The scale is at the top. 1 means that this particular trait is unlike you, and 7 means that this is very much like you. At this point, fill out the test. Your instructor will later tell you how to score the test. Remember that an androgynous person is no better or worse than a person with more traditional concepts of gender. It does seem important for a person to become aware of their beliefs about sex-roles and have tolerance for others' beliefs. It also seems wise that an androgynous person marry an androgynous person because they will have similar expectations for each other.

LEARNING ACTIVITIES

1	2	3	4	5	6	7
Never or almost never true	Usually not true	Sometimes but infrequently	Occasionally true	Often true	Usually true	Always or almost always true

- Self reliant
- Yielding
- Helpful
- Defends own beliefs
- Cheerful
- Moody
- Independent
- Shy
- Conscientious
- Athletic
- Affectionate
- Theatrical
- Assertive
- Flatterable
- Happy
- Strong personality
- Loyal
- Unpredictable
- Forceful
- Feminine

- Reliable
- Analytical
- Sympathetic
- Jealous
- Has leadership ability
- Sensitive to the needs of others
- Truthful
- Willing to take risks
- Understanding
- Secretive
- Makes decisions easily
- Compassionate
- Sincere
- Self-sufficient
- Eager to soothe hurt feelings
- Conceited
- Dominant
- Soft-spoken
- Likable
- Masculine

- Warm
- Solemn
- Willing to take a stand
- Tender
- Friendly
- Aggressive
- Gullible
- Inefficient
- Acts as a leader
- Childlike
- Adaptable
- Individualistic
- Does not use harsh language
- Unsystematic
- Competitive
- Loves Children
- Tactful
- Ambitious
- Gentle
- Conventional

169

A SELF-ESTEEM INVENTORY

If the statement describes how you usually feel, put a check in the column, "Like Me". If the statement does not describe how you usually feel, put a check in the column, "Unlike Me". (Note: There are no right or wrong answers)

		Like Me	Unlike Me
1.	I spend a lot of time daydreaming.	____	____
2.	I'm pretty sure of myself.	____	____
3.	I often wish I were someone else.	____	____
4.	I'm pretty easy to like.	____	____
5.	My parents and I have a lot of fun together.	____	____
6.	I never worry about anything.	____	____
7.	I find it very hard to talk in front of the class.	____	____
8.	I wish I were younger.	____	____
9.	I would change a lot of things about myself if I could.	____	____
10.	I can make up my own mind.	____	____
11.	I'm fun to be with.	____	____
12.	I get upset easily at home.	____	____
13.	I always do the right thing.	____	____
14.	I'm proud of my school work.	____	____
15.	Someone always has to tell me what to do.	____	____
16.	It takes me a long time to get used to anything new.	____	____
17.	I'm often sorry for things I do.	____	____
18.	I'm popular with kids my own age.	____	____

19. My parents usually consider my feelings.   ⎯⎯   ⎯⎯

20. I'm never happy.   ⎯⎯   ⎯⎯

21. I'm doing the best work I can.   ⎯⎯   ⎯⎯

22. I give in very easily.   ⎯⎯   ⎯⎯

23. I can usually take care of myself.   ⎯⎯   ⎯⎯

24. I'm pretty happy.   ⎯⎯   ⎯⎯

YOUR STYLE OF LEARNING AND THINKING
Right, Left, or Whole Brain Dominance

1. Count the "A's" in the items that end with the numbers 1, 2, 3, 4, 5 (11, 12, ... 21, 22, ... 31, 32, ... etc.) _____

2. Count the "B's" in the items that end with the numbers 6, 7, 8, 9, 0 (16, 17, ... 26, 27, ... 36, 37, ... etc.) _____

3. Count the "A's" in the items that end with the numbers 6, 7, 8, 9, 0. _____

4. Count the "B's" in the items that end with the numbers 1, 2, 3, 4, 5. _____

5. Count all of the "C's". This is your whole brain score. _____

6. Add the totals from lines 1 and 2 above. This is your left brain score. _____

7. Add the totals from lines 3 and 4 above. This is your right brain score. _____

8. Subtract right brain from left brain. It can be a minus or a plus number. _____

9. If your whole brain score is 15 or higher, divide your answer in line 8 by 3. Round to the nearest number. The answer will be your score. It can be a plus or minus number. _____

10. If your whole brain score is from 9-14, divide your answer in line 8 by 2. This is your score. _____

11. If your whole brain score is less than 9, do not divide at all. This is your score. _____

INTERPERSONAL REASONING

Thinking about yourself in relationship to another person is called interpersonal reasoning. The ability to be successful at it implies that we reason well about ourselves and understand how our thoughts and feelings might be similar or dissimilar to those of other people. This competence permits us to observe our behavior and another's behavior as part of a relationship experience.

Not everyone is equally skillful at doing it. But some skill appears, on the surface, to be a part of all satisfying relationships. Likewise, inadequacy to reason well may contribute to diminished satisfaction.

The development of interpersonal reasoning appears to depend in part on the use of language. When parents use "I - Thou" language (e.g. "I love you" and "It seems to me you are unhappy"), children learn to use it as part of their routine verbal expression. Early words and behavioral referents for the words then allow an individual to gradually expand vocabulary, and improve and refine observational skills.

Being able to gather observations about interpersonal behavior enables us to infer what one's actions may mean. After observing someone's facial expression and vocal tone, we could say and infer something about their feelings which we cannot directly see. When we infer or guess correctly, our judgements are reinforced and we feel more adequate to predict other interpersonal events. Those capable of observing and inferring the most accurately about themselves and others will usually find greater reward in social experiences. Misjudgment resulting from inadequate observations and inaccurate inferences, obviously may lead to increased conflict and dissatisfaction.

One can readily understand why interpersonal reasoning is closely tied to any given language culture. We use words to symbolize observable and unobserveable interpersonal events. Most know and appreciate that words of one language do not literally translate to words of another. The subtleties of the words in any language often cannot be accurately understood before one has had extensive practice.

The expression of love, for example, is an interpersonal event. Yet, how it is expressed and observed might differ from person to person because of different experiences.

How We Can Influence the Development of Interpersonal Reasoning

Children can benefit from any focused attempt to enrich their learning. Parents can enhance children's ability to reason interpersonally by increasing the amount of time they think and learn about the social world. When children are participants in varieties of social experiences and have discussion opportunities about them, they can observe more accurately. When these are tested and reinforced, skill increases as they anticipate future rewards.

Other effective ways children learn to reason about interpersonal behavior is through imitation, games, and social play. These activities allow practice in a more secure situation. The true to life imitations however, sharpen observational skills and improve the inferences children can make about them.

STAGES OF DEVELOPMENT

The Proving Age 0-6	Children gather information from the family and other social environments. Preliminary tests are made to learn which assumption can be relied on. Their ability to make inferences about social conditions is limited by the amount of experience and children's sense of ego centrism.
Social Inferences Ages 7-12	At age six children can infer that someone's thoughts might differ from their own. By age eight, children know that others can understand them. By age ten, children can distinguish between what others think from what they think about something.
Refinement Age 13-	Increased varieties of social experience and attempts to validate what is observed leads a continual refinement of interpersonal reasoning. Individuals begin to apply their reasoning skills to specific areas of interest and need such as heterosexual relationships and work environments.

LEARNING ACTIVITIES

Activity I: What causes your actions

Purpose: To enable students to identify internal or external causes of their own behavior.

1. Describe how you have acted in the following situations and the sequence of events leading up to them.
    a. when you were angry _____
    b. when you were rejected by someone _____
    c. when you failed at some task _____
    d. when you love someone _____
    e. when you are depressed _____

2. For each description identify what you believe caused your response. _____
_____
_____
_____
_____

3. Answer: Do you tend to think you cause your actions through your own choices or are your actions caused by conditions external to you. _____

4. What do you believe are the consequences for a person who is internally controlled as compared to someone who is externally controlled? _____
_____
_____
_____

Activity II: Improving Your Interpersonal Reasoning

Purpose: To help students improve observational and inference skills.

1. During a routine day, imitate someone's walk, another person's style of talk, posture while sitting, and hand gestures while speaking.

2. Play a game of charades with the following social situations.
    a. a rejected lover
    b. an excited teenager
    c. an angry policeman
    d. a stuffy professor
    e. an excited conversation

   f. an angry conversation
   g. an obligated conversation

3. Interview four people and ask them to describe the following types of behavior. Determine how much of the four subjects agree.
   a. an embarrassed person
   b. an insecure person
   c. an unloved person
   d. an unhappy person

4. Write a paper which records all the results of these activities.

DEVELOPMENT OF ADOLESCENT PEER GROUPS

No study of adolescence in American society would be complete without understanding the development of adolescent peer groups. Membership in peer groups is part of nearly everyone's experience during adolescence and often exerts great influence on us.

The basis for peer groups is probably the social and emotional need to take a small step away from home-like conditions and establish an identity with same age individuals. Most adolescents have similar emotional and social needs which provides the motivation for them to join together as a means of finding satisfaction. By studying about adolescent peer groups we can increase our understanding of the adolescent period of life.

There are three general types of group membership that adolescents create. These may be real or imaginary. Youth think about an imaginary group which serves as an "audience" for their social behavior. Parents know this group by the name of "they." A teen may say, "they all are going," or "they are wearing this style of clothing." Youth also join groups that serve as "models" for them to emulate one another which critically evaluates their performances.

All social groups have rules of membership and exert pressure for individuals to comply with them. These may be informal or formal such as a style of dress, use of new vocabulary, loyalty oaths, and/or time involvement. Failure to satisfy these rules may result in an individual being excluded. Since acceptance usually is a strong motive, the threat of exclusion often places an individual under considerable amounts of pressure to comply. This is one of the reasons why peer groups exert great influence on adolescents.

The composition of peer groups and the types of participation change as children mature and become more socially aware. Same sex groups are the first to form. Members come together to serve a common task or because they are in similar geographical locations. This first stage is followed by membership in groups which allows individuals to perform social tasks such as meet members of the other sex and promote status in the larger social networks of school, church, and community. Heterosexual groups form in the next stage with higher status members beginning to date. Generally members of these groups have similar socio-economic backgrounds and are organized similar to levels of status in their community. The last stage of peer groups consists of dating pairs who balance time between dating alone and with other member paris. Eventually time and commitment to the group wanes and couples pair up and begin shared living arrangements.

HOW GROUP MEMBERSHIP HELPS CHILDREN DEVELOP

Peer groups are the chief means by which children are helped to move away from parental ties and achieve independence. In our society they provide opportunities for individuals to gradually participate in society. Group membership gives individuals opportunities to gather information about themselves which can be used to promote one's identity.

Because these two useful purposes are accomplished by group membership, parents and others involved with child care can ensure that children have a positive experience. More open and free communication with parents can help children select groups that provide fun and positive social experiences. Parents can, for example, become acquainted with their own children's friends and communicate support for them to be together. This may also require parents to adjust family rules to allow for increased flexibility. Rather than fear those changes in the family, parents can view them as part of the process which eventually will result in child independence. Further, parents can engage their children in formulating steps toward increased independence and place themselves in a position of support rather than that of indifference and restriction.

It is well known, of course, that many parents find their adolescent children in peer groups that do not reflect their family's values. This is made more likely by the presence of conflict in the home and/or weak family ties. When this situation exists it presents difficulty for all involve. The adolescent, however, is usually the one person who is most adversely affected because he or she is the one developing and changing. Conflict between parents and children that involves peers is unsettling and disrupting at this time in life when important developmental tasks could be accomplished. Conflict can delay personality development and/or alter its form. Adolescents can and perhaps should be informed of the importance selection of groups can have for them.

LEARNING ACTIVITIES

Activity I: <u>Survey of Sources of Information for Adolescents</u>

Purpose: To enable students to determine the sources of learning used by them during adolescence.

Instructions:

1. Complete the following survey to identify the source of learning for 30 types of knowledge.

2. Summarize the results by finding whether you learned more from parents, relatives, yourself, or friends.

3. Evaluate the amount of success you believe you had during the years of 12-18. Do you believe the sources of information you used contributed to the amount of success you experienced? Why or why not?

Inventory of Adolescent Experiences

Part 1

The items in this section describe various types of success. Read each one carefully and then indicate whether it describes you. If it does, mark "yes." If the statement does not describe you, mark "no." If the statement is only partly accurate then mark "partly true."

A. I have developed one or more talents such as sports, music, mechanics, and have received recognition for it.
    YES   NO   PARTLY TRUE

B. I have enjoyed several close friends who really seem to like me.
    YES   NO   PARTLY TRUE

C. I have learned good work habits and can usually accomplish whatever I want.
    YES   NO   PARTLY TRUE

D. I feel confident about my abilities nearly all the time.
    YES   NO   PARTLY TRUE

E. I have received recognition for my achievements.
    YES   NO   PARTLY TRUE

F. I have had a fun and successful time dating.
    YES   NO   PARTLY TRUE

G. My relationship with my parents and family has been satisfactory.
    YES   NO   PARTLY TRUE

H. I have demonstrated an ability to learn and am excited about learning new things.
    YES   NO   PARTLY TRUE

I. I have avoided committing any criminal offense.
    YES   NO   PARTLY TRUE

J. Except for minor illnesses or injuries, I have been quite healthy.
    YES   NO   PARTLY TRUE

K. I know what I value and can choose between what I value and what I do not.
    YES   NO   PARTLY TRUE

L. I have avoided much contact with drugs and alcohol.
    YES   NO   PARTLY TRUE

M. I am generally considerate of others and do not make snap judgements.
    YES   NO   PARTLY TRUE

Part 2

Statements listed below describe things people can learn while growing up. After reading each one carefully, indicate whether you learned it from you father, you mother, your friends, your relatives (such as aunt or uncle), or by yourself. Circle the appropriate one. In cases where you might have learned something from more than one source, check the one that contributed the most to your knowledge.

	Types of Learning	Sources of Learning (Circle one)				
1.	Work Habits	Father	Mother	Friends	Relatives	Myself
2.	Information about sex	Father	Mother	Friends	Relatives	Myself
3.	How to make friends	Father	Mother	Friends	Relatives	Myself
4.	Ways to develop my talents	Father	Mother	Friends	Relatives	Myself
5.	What to pursue as a career	Father	Mother	Friends	Relatives	Myself
6.	My desire for an education	Father	Mother	Friends	Relatives	Myself
7.	My ability to communicate with others	Father	Mother	Friends	Relatives	Myself
8.	Expressing affection to others	Father	Mother	Friends	Relatives	Myself
9.	My ability to organize and plan	Father	Mother	Friends	Relatives	Myself
10.	My negative feelings about myself	Father	Mother	Friends	Relatives	Myself
11.	How to have successful dates	Father	Mother	Friends	Relatives	Myself
12.	How I keep my personal appearance	Father	Mother	Friends	Relatives	Myself
13.	My beliefs about God	Father	Mother	Friends	Relatives	Myself
14.	How to overcome personal problems	Father	Mother	Friends	Relatives	Myself
15.	How honest I am	Father	Mother	Friends	Relatives	Myself
16.	My belief about the importance of obeying the law	Father	Mother	Friends	Relatives	Myself
17.	My ability to express my thoughts	Father	Mother	Friends	Relatives	Myself
18.	My taste in clothes	Father	Mother	Friends	Relatives	Myself
19.	How aware I am of other people's feelings	Father	Mother	Friends	Relatives	Myself
20.	Poor eating habits	Father	Mother	Friends	Relatives	Myself
21.	My hobbies	Father	Mother	Friends	Relatives	Myself
22.	How I control my temper	Father	Mother	Friends	Relatives	Myself
23.	Courtesy towards others	Father	Mother	Friends	Relatives	Myself
24.	Good eating manners and habits	Father	Mother	Friends	Relatives	Myself
25.	My positive feelings about myself	Father	Mother	Friends	Relatives	Myself
26.	How dishonest I am	Father	Mother	Friends	Relatives	Myself
27.	My attitudes toward the opposite sex	Father	Mother	Friends	Relatives	Myself
28.	Being critical of others	Father	Mother	Friends	Relatives	Myself
29.	Attitudes I have about people	Father	Mother	Friends	Relatives	Myself
30.	My religious practices	Father	Mother	Friends	Relatives	Myself

Activity II: <u>Evaluation of adolescent Groups</u>

Purpose: To enable students to evaluate the groups they joined from 12-13 years of age.

Instructions:

1. Identify the types of groups in your high school (e.g., preppies, jocks, etc.) Answer the following questions about them:
   a. What were the identifying characteristics of each group?
   b. What type of reputation did each group have?
   c. How did these groups influence individuals?
   d. What were people's motives for joining a group?

2. List all clubs, organizations, or groups of friends in which you were a member between the years 12-18. Answer the following questions:
   a. What were the rules of membership for each group?
   b. What were your reasons for joining?
   c. Which groups had values similar to those of your parents?
   d. Which groups had values conflicting with your parents values?
   e. Which groups exerted the greatest influence on you?
   f. If you were not a member of any group, what were these effects on you?

ACHIEVEMENT MOTIVATION

Unless impaired in some way, all infants show a remarkable motivation to learn and improve. It is expressed in the intense efforts infants make to creep, crawl, walk, and run. All physical, social, and psychological development during infancy can be traced in part to this motivation.

Since this is present in virtually every young child it is reasonable that later on children would apply it to achievement other than developmental tasks. These may include improvement of talents, academic performance, and some social skills. Behavioral scientists have labeled this motivation as <u>achievement motivation</u>.

After infancy, this motivation is not present in all children to the same degree. It seems reasonable to assume that some events or experiences must have taken place to inhibit the expression of achievement motivation. It may also be the case that the original sense of competency received such little reinforcement that other adaptations were learned.

The literature describing the development of achievement motivation clearly and consistently suggests that it is the result of individuals (e.g. parents) and social environments actively promoting it (McClelland, 1955; DeCharms and Moeller, 1962).

This means that achievement motivation is the result of a child's actions combined with what parents, school teachers, and other acquaintances might contribute. When this is not accomplished, children are said to develop a <u>fear of failure</u> which on the surface appears to be somewhat like achievement motivation, but as we shall see, is quite different.

Achievement motivation is characterized by positive attitudes about the task, moderate amounts of tension (working tension), a clear belief that the person can succeed at the task, organized efforts, and persistence to completion of the task. Fear of failure is, in contrast to achievement motivation, characterized by an extreme intensity about a task or by passivity. Further, tasks are faced with apprehension and a genuine fear that failure, not success, will take place. In extreme cases, fear of failure is so intense that performance is impaired. An example is test anxiety that reduces students' levels of performance because of the mental blocks it creates.

HOW TO DEVELOP ACHIEVEMENT MOTIVATION

Learning to achieve requires two mental abilities which include the ability to organize and define success (goals) and the ability to maintain energy levels high enough to impel action and low enough to permit an adequate response. Defining success is learned when children are shown exactly what to do, encouraged to do well, and rewarded when the task is complete. When this sequence is repeated many times throughout childhood, it becomes an individual's way of approaching any performance.

Interestingly, this sequence is learned more effectively when a child is started on a task, then left alone while supervised in alternating sequences. As children mature, external rewards are supplanted by satisfaction that stems from doing what is predicted. True achievement motivation is predicting the level of performance then achieving it.

The ability to regulate energy or the arousal part of achievement motivation is both learned and based on inherited characteristics. Children appear to reduce high arousal and increase low arousal. Apparently, everyone has an individual range of energy that contributes to optimal performance. This tendency seems to appear in all primates, suggesting it is inherited. The actual range of variation, however, seems to be affected by learning. A child reared in a calm environment may have a different range of optimal arousal than one who has experienced excessive amounts of extreme emotions. Ironically, the experience of extreme emotions tends to reduce the optimal energy range.

Graphically, the level of arousal, related to achievement motivation is termed a butterfly curve. The center line is called an adaptation level (the level of arousal normally experienced) and the distance between the arrow is the optimal range of arousal. As arousal increases or decreases to the highest point on the curve, motivation and achievement is optimal. If arousal levels are above or below, the level of performance diminishes.

The role of learning in achievement motivation stems largely from the types of activities children are taught to use in reducing or increasing arousal. As part of child care, for example, parents may put a child on a chair or in an isolated situation to reduce arousal. Children can use an inner dialogue to alter emotional states. The presence of other people either in cooperation or as an audience may affect arousal levels. Children may learn to anticipate a reward for performing if consequences are positive, or they may fear guilt if consequences are too punitive. Positive consequences over time, yield a less extreme range of arousal, while guilt from punitive consequences tend to create arousal so extreme that performance levels are reduced. This is the aforementioned condition termed fear of failure.

LEARNING ACTIVITIES

Activity I: Predicting Success

Purpose: To help students to practice developing success expectations for tasks they perform.

Instructions:

1. During a period of one week, select three tasks that you are required to perform. Prior to beginning each, spend two minutes thinking about the following: a) what is your standard of success for each task, b) how you will feel when you succeed at each task, and c) the many possible (imagine many) rewards that will come from being successful.

2. Record the amount of time to complete each task and describe your reaction when you finished.

3. Select two other tasks you are required to perform. Prior to beginning each task spend two minutes thinking about the following ideas: a) identify the reasons why you might fail in your attempts, b) what are the awful consequences for failure, c) imagine the disapproval, pain, and other punishments that could result from your failure.

4. Record the amount of time required to complete each of the two tasks and describe your reactions if you finish or do not finish.

Activity II: External or Internal Pressure

Purpose: To help students identify whether the sources of arousal energy are internal or external.

Instructions:

1. Write a brief performance autobiography which covers the last eight years of your life. In your writing, identify tasks you performed. These should include school achievement, chores at home, part- or full-time work, development of personal talents and/or skills (i.e. athletics, music, art).

2. Examine each achievement in terms of the following criteria. a) Type of motivation means whether you achieved largely because you were self-directed or because external pressure was placed on you. b) Type of rewards for achieving includes intrinsic rewards of happiness and feelings of success and extrinsic rewards of money, praise, or prizes. c) Length of duration means

whether or not you are still performing and plan to continue performing the task (indicate "continuing" or "not continuing").

3. After completing the chart, evaluate whether you have learned to achieve internally or externally and determine if the method you have learned seems to determine the length of time you plan on continuing the task.

Achievement	Type of Motivation	Types of Reward	Length of duration
1.			
2.			
3.			
4.			
5.			
6.			
7.			

DEVELOPMENT OF ACHIEVEMENT MOTIVATION

Arousal Reduction 0-2	After birth, children seek arousal reducing activities. Until the age of two, achievement is a result of maturation and reflexive responses including motor activities and cognitive growth.
Arousal Increase and Exploration 3-6	Children begin to increase arousal by exploring more and satisfying curiosity drive. Arousal levels begin to be randomly tied to satisfaction of discovery and performance.
Integration of Arousal and Performance 7-12	Children tie strategies of arousal reduction and increase to performance tasks. School, chores at home, and social events are sources of learning. Positive or punitive reactions of other people to children's performance influence children's arousal levels. Encouragement and rewards lead to higher levels of achievement motivation.
Performance and Prediction 13-18	Children further refine achievement motivation by developing predictions about their performance. Those high in achievement motivation take intermediate risks and adjust downward on second attempts if they fail on first efforts. Those low in achievement motivation either take no risks or excessive risks. Failure is responded to by an exaggerated prediction, usually upward from previous predictions. Failure produces increased arousal, and children believe they must do more on subsequent attempts to compensate for the first failure. These characteristics become highly stylized and long term traits appear to be established.

BIBLIOGRAPHY

Becker, W.C. "Consequences of Different Kinds of Parental Discipline." In M.L. Hoffman and L.W. Hoffman (Eds.) *Review of Child Development Research*. Vol. 1. New York: Russell Sage, 1964. Pp. 169-208.

Boyce, W.D., and Jensen, L.C., *Moral Reasoning: A Psychological-Philosophical Interaction*. University of Nebraska Press, 1978.

Decharms, R. and Moeller, G.H., "Values Expressed in American Children's Readers: 1800-1950," *Journal of Abnormal and Social Psychology*, 1962, 64, 136-142.

Ekman, P. "Primary Emotions" *Psychology Today*, March, 1985.

Gagne, R.M., *The Conditions of Learning* (Third Edition). New York: Holt, Rinehart, and Winston, 1977.

Garvey, C., *Play (The Development Child Series)*. Cambridge, Mass: Harvard University Press, 1977.

Harter, S., "Developmental Differences in the Manifestation of Mastery Motivation on Problem-Solving Tasks," *Child Development*, 1975, 46(2), 370-378.

Helms, D.B., and Turner, J.S., *Lifespan Development* (Second Edition). New York: Holt, Rinehart, and Winston, 1983.

Kellerman, H. "An Epigenetic Theory of Emotions in Early Development" in *Emotion: Theory, Research, and Experience* (Ed. Plutchik and Kellerman), 1984.

Kohlberg, L., "The Development of Children's Orientations Towards a Moral Order: I. Sequence in the Development of Human Thought," *Vita Human*, 1963, 6, 11-33.

LeFrancois, G.R., *Of Children*. Belmont, Calif: Wadsworth 1980.

LeFrancois, G.R., *Psychology*. Belmont, Calif: Wadsworth 1980.

McClelland, D.C., "Some Social Consequences of Achievement Motivation," in M.R. Jones (Ed.) *Nebraska Symposium on Motivation* (Vol. 3), Lincoln: University of Nebraska Press, 1955.

Montemayer, R. and Eisen, M., "The Development of Self-Conceptions From Childhood to Adolescence," *Developmental Psychology*, 1977, 13, 314-19.

Nelson, K., "Structure and Strategy in Learning to Talk" <u>Monographs for the Society for Research in Child Development</u>, 1973, (Serial No. 149) 38 (1-2).

Plutchik, R. <u>Emotion: A Psychoevolutionary Synthesis</u>. New York, New York: Harper and Row, 1980.

Schoolar, J.C., <u>Current Issues in Adolescent Psychiatry</u>, Chapter One, "Normal Adolescence in Perspective" by Offer, D. and Offer, J. Institute for Psychosomatic and Psychiatric Research and Training, Michael Reese Hospital and Pritzker School of Medicine, University of Chicago.

Selman, R.L., and Selman, A.P., "Children's Ideas About Friendship: A New Theory," <u>Psychology Today</u>, 1979, 13(4), 71-80, 114.

Stevens, S. <u>The Learning Disabled Child: Ways that Parents Can Help</u> John F. Blair Publishers, Winston-Salem, NC 1980.

Thomas, A. and Chess, S. <u>Temperament and Development</u>. 1977. New York: Brunner/Mazel.

Vandell, D.L., Wilson, K.S., and Buchanan, N.R., "Peer Interaction in the First Year of Life: An Examination of Structure, Content, and Sensitivity to Toys," <u>Child Development</u>, 1980, 51, 481-488.

Vygotsky, L.S., <u>Thought and Language</u>. Cambridge: MIT Press, 1962.